UNFU[CK]
YOUR
STRESS

Using Science to Cope with Distress and Embrace Excitement

Dr. Faith G. Harper, LPC-S, ACS, ACN

Microcosm Publishing
Portland, Ore | Cleveland, Ohio

UNFUCK YOUR STRESS: Using Science to Cope with Distress and Embrace Excitement

© Dr. Faith G. Harper, 2023

First edition - 5,000 copies - October 10, 2023

ISBN 978-1-64841-257-8

This is Microcosm #803

Edited by Olivia Rollins
Cover and design by Joe Biel
This edition © Microcosm Publishing, 2023
For a catalog, write or visit:
Microcosm Publishing
2752 N Williams Ave.
Portland, OR 97227

www.Microcosm.Pub/Stress

Library of Congress Cataloging-in-Publication Data

MICROCOSM · PUBLISHING

Microcosm Publishing is Portland's most diversified publishing house and distributor, with a focus on the colorful, authentic, and empowering. Our books and zines have put your power in your hands since 1996, equipping readers to make positive changes in their lives and in the world around them. Microcosm emphasizes skill-building, showing hidden histories, and fostering creativity through challenging conventional publishing wisdom with books and bookettes about DIY skills, food, bicycling, gender, self-care, and social justice. What was once a distro and record label started by Joe Biel in a drafty bedroom was determined to be *Publishers Weekly*'s fastest-growing publisher of 2022 and #3 in 2023, and is now among the oldest independent publishing houses in Portland, OR, and Cleveland, OH. We are a politically moderate, centrist publisher in a world that has inched to the right for the past 80 years.

TABLE OF CONTENTS

....

Introduction

Stress is not a new cultural crisis by any means. And struggling with stress doesn't make you a whiney titty baby who just needs to suck it up, no matter what the hot productivity coach of the moment is saying on social media about biohacking or whatever. It *is* true that the construct we call stress has become entrenched in the cultural miasma, which I'm super good with. Talking about what we are noticing is a really important start. Because how else does real change take place? All that is to say that stress sucks. It has always sucked. No one enjoys stress, big or small. It wears us out, whether it's finding out your building is for sale and you have to move in a month or finding out someone jacked your lunch from the break room fridge.

And it isn't just the product of colonialism and industrialization.[1] Versions of stressful situations have existed throughout human history. No feudal serf thought life was fabulous, I'm willing to wager. But only in more recent times have we come to better understand how stress is a true body-mind assault that everyone has to contend with at some (most) points and in some (most) areas of their lives. Media does love

---

1 Though I am down with dismantling both to see if it helps.

a good clickbaity headline, and alarmist news about stress is everywhere. We've all seen those pictures and videos taken of the midsections of people on the street with a voiceover speaking in Very Concerned Tones (™) about stress causing more belly fat.[2]

Something those headlines don't always tell us is that stress is not the external event (that would be a *stressor*, if you are keeping up with your Scrabble dictionary); stress is our response to external events (good, bad, or neutral) based on ever-shifting factors, both internal and external. Like, getting stuck in a long line at the coffee shop is stressful. Especially if you are in a car queue and can't escape and you are now going to be late to work. Your stress response could come from feeling trapped, being fearful of getting written up for being late, etc. You could react by tensing up and thinking, "This is it, no way am I getting that promotion now . . . hell, I bet my desk will be emptied into a box when I get there." Or you could shrug to yourself and think "I'll order a snack for my boss to butter them up over my lateness, and in the meantime, the new episode of *You're Wrong About* just dropped, so I'll listen to that while I chill here for longer than expected."

Which isn't to say the first reaction is bad or wrong. As we will talk about in this book ad nauseam, our stress responses become grooved patterns based on a lot of different factors, and a negative response may be a perfectly logical one to have. Though this isn't a "shit's fucked" statement of hopelessness. Knowledge is fucking power in this regard, because knowing what's going on is a really important part of coping with stress and even transforming it where possible.

---

2 If you are a producer please stop this shit. It's shady, lazy b-roll work, not to mention completely unkind to people who live in larger bodies.

So this book is gonna start with a little bit of stress school. We're going to learn about the history of scientific inquiry around stress and the different forms it can take. And for my fellow science nerds, we are then going to do a hella science deep dive. We're going to talk about the physiological science of stress with lots of vagus nerve nerdacity. We're going to talk about where and when stress is actually considered a diagnosable condition (short version: when it's trauma related). We're going to talk about chronic stress, survival mode, imposter syndrome, and burnout, which is another construct that is both common and misunderstood. Why these heavier topics instead of the usual "put your keys in the same place every day when you get home so you don't find them in the freezer after being hella late to school the next day because they were missing"? Because you can stop assigning a college professor classes to teach, but you can't stop her from teaching. But also, because it's really important to consider how a pile-up of small things causes larger issues, even changing our brain function over time and leading to things like trauma responses.

Which also means we are going to discuss how to figure out if your particular stressors require functional coping strategies or transformational ones, and then we're going to go deep into the coping strategies themselves (this is a huge part of the book, because we all need as many tools for dealing with stress as we can possibly get). And finally, we're going to look at stress in the context of relationships. As always, the tools I share in this book are the ones that I have used most successfully in my own clinical work. Ready? Stoodis.

How to Use This Book

As I hinted above, this book has two parts. The first part is the history-and-science part I already threatened you with. The second is all about how to cope with stress, meaning it gives you the tools to help you either brace for impact, heal from impact, or avoid impact. Also, if you are a regular reader of my books and zines and articles and the like, there will be stuff in here you have seen before. Part of the goal of this book was to collect together all my previous writings about stress while adding in some more juicy details.

And while every single one of my books has some kind of "how to use this book" section, I remain terrible at writing them. Because I am a member of Generation X, which means I fully support you using the book however you see fit. Jump around if you like, the book won't break if you read it backwards (tho watch for accidental spellcasting so you don't accidentally summon a Demogorgon). Read it and use it to drunkenly lecture others at closing time. Or just read what applies to you, find stuff that's helpful, and move on with your life. It's all good.

Tho if you do accidentally summon a Demogorgon, I need to see pictures and know which section of the book read backwards led to that particular outcome.

Part One:
How Stress
Works

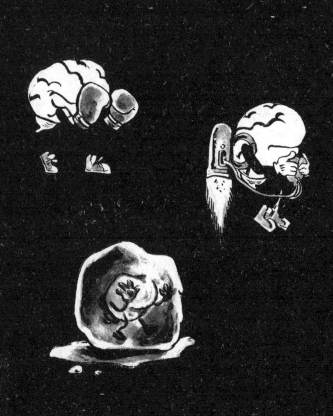

CHAPTER 1:
WHAT IS STRESS?

Stress affects us all differently. Some people thrive on it and use that energy to get shit done. Others feel overwhelmed and check out. Maybe you get energized and motivated. Maybe your shoulders get tight. Maybe your whole body gets tight. Maybe you yell at people or drive recklessly. Maybe you space out. We all respond differently based on our previous experiences. But before we can understand our individual responses, we need to know a little background. So we're going to start there, by learning about the history of stress and exploring some of the ways that stress can manifest in our lives.

The History of Stress

The idea of stress is so normal in current society, it seems impossible that the concept of stress as a psychological phenomenon is relatively new. And while it is a ubiquitous term, it's also a very fuzzy one. It could mean processing traumatic events or dealing with debilitating disease. Or it could mean having a huge assignment due or getting stuck in the pick-up lane at your kids' school. And while no one is trying to state that all these experiences are equal, they all have a tendency to fall under the umbrella of "stress."

Now, the idea of stress existed way earlier, at least as far back as the Roman Empire, and referred to how different forces act on an object. Like the weight that goes over a bridge or whatever. The word "stress" itself comes from the Latin word *strictus*, referencing how something tightens or constricts. Eventually the idea of stress carried over to humans (in about the 16th century), and the term "distress" was born. But the focus was on how the world around us impacts our physical body, so essentially injury or harm.

What about mental/emotional/psychological harm? The idea of "stress" within that domain started with the work of Claude Bernard, best known as a father of experimental medicine. He was a pretty big whoop at the time, positing theories that have since borne out but were pretty radical. Western thinking about the human body up until that point was that all organs operated independently. But here was Doc Bernard already figuring stuff out about vagal tone and the like, referencing the human body as "the environment within," and discussing how this environment is designed to maintain a level of homeostasis.

Around the same time, pathologist Sir William Osler pointed out that cognitions (specifically our attitude) played a role in our health outcomes. Both of these gentlemen made important observations that everyone said "eh, maybe" to and then promptly forgot about for many more decades.

But then Walter Cannon came along. He was into both experimental psych and physiology. He was also heavily influenced by being sent to France (along with a medical unit from Harvard) to study what was then termed *shell shock*, which we now know as *post-traumatic stress disorder*. The military was confused by the symptoms,[3] which didn't seem to correlate with a visible physical injury. Some clinicians thought these psychological symptoms were the result of a traumatic brain injury, and they were kinda right but not in the way they thought. PTSD is, essentially, a form of acquired neurodiversity just like a traumatic brain injury. But that made it more complicated for the military, because they wanted the affected soldiers treated quickly so they could be returned to combat instead of discharged.

Back then Cannon didn't even use the term "stress," but instead referred to what he was seeing as *disturbances* of our physiological responses. The idea pissed off the military so much that they banned the term "shell shock," thinking that if the term didn't exist neither would the condition.[4]

Cannon wasn't the only one to call bullshit. He started using the term "stress" in 1935, along with Hans Selye, who I've written about before because his ineptitude with injections on lab rats taught him about the endocrinological components of stress.[5]

Then, in 1945, Roy Grinker and John Spiegel, also tired of military-industrial-complex shenanigans, published their book *Men Under Stress*, which was about the cumulative effects of

3 Though they shouldn't have been . . . we have reports of PTSD experienced by soldiers throughout the history of humans making reports. The symptoms have always been consistent; it's only the language that is different. The term flashback comes from the motion picture industry, because it's a conceit used in movies to demonstrate the past hijacking the present. Civil War veterans, for example, referenced being visited or haunted by ghosts. Same thing.
4 I'm fucking SERIOUS, y'all. These assbananas thought soldiers were malingering and making up their PTSD.
5 He was trying to study the effects of ovarian extracts on rats but sucked horribly at the injections. He kept dropping the rats and ended up chasing them around the laboratory for hours on end. Fortunately, he was a far better physiologist than rat handler, and he noticed that his ineptness was causing enlarged adrenal glands, fucked-up immune systems, and ulcers in all of the rats that were fried by his continuous bullshit.

soldiers being in incredibly fucked-up situations for enormous amounts of time and how it often doesn't get better once they get home. Keep in mind, the idea of traumatic stress still made military officials plug their fingers in their ears and scream "lalalalaLA can't hear you!" until Vietnam veterans organized and petitioned for PTSD to be added to *The Diagnostic and Statistical Manual of Mental Disorders* (DSM) in nineteen-fucking-eighty.

So up until this point, stress research and observational reports were centered on *traumatic stress*, the precursor to PTSD. It wasn't until after WWII[6] that the idea of stress was expanded in Western society as a label for the wibbly-wobbly, timey-wimey combination of psychological and physiological responses that we display when we hit the tipping point of *too much* and/or *out of balance*.

Now, there are cranky people out there who say, "Ugh, stress is such a bullshit modern concept . . . our ancestors had it far worse." I mean, maybe. They definitely couldn't soothe their souls with a new magazine and an iced coffee. But I'm writing this in 2023, and while the plagues and the attacks from warring factions are maybe higher tech, they aren't *that* much different from what our earliest ancestors experienced.

And yes, how we define and operationalize stress has changed over time, making it a protean concept. But that's true of most everything as we learn more about the mind-body interaction. And the concept being a newer one doesn't make it untrue. It isn't a made-up TikTok diagnosis. The physiology of stress has been demonstrated over and over again as a real thing that impacts the body in real ways. Does paying attention to our metacognitions about stress matter? Of course it does; there is

---

6 At which point we can no longer call it shell shock, so it's "battle fatigue."

much we can do to mitigate and/or manage our responses. But to say we're being soft and weak is some bullshit. Please remember that the expression "pulling oneself up by one's bootstraps" was a sarcastic saying meant to describe something that is literally impossible. No one can do any of this alone.

Stress vs. Distress

So stress is bad? According to Doktor Hans it is, but further scientific inquiry demonstrates that it is a bit more complex than that. Which, of course. Welcome to being human.

Our bodies are quite able to manage occasional stressors and have a nice orderly way of doing so. But as Selye discovered through his dumbass behavior, our bodies are not designed to respond to stress all the fucking time. When that happens our bodies get overloaded and we get sick. Selye referred to this overload as *general adaptation syndrome*, which today is called "adrenal fatigue."

But in a clinical sense, *stress* is a more neutral term that refers to *any event that requires an output of resources*.

Stress can be good (output of resources to create art, run a race, or finish school) or it can be bad (output of resources to cope with a car accident, an illness, or being terminated from a job). What determines whether something is good or bad? We do. Good means it is in service of an outcome we want, bad means we are coping with something we don't want. Kelly McGonigal, in her book *The Upside of Stress*, defines stress in terms of meaning. Things are stressful to us because they fucking matter to us. Which also means we can *sometimes* change our stress responses by changing our framing without self-gaslighting or spiritual bypassing. And we will get more into that in a bit. But first, let's unpack some more physiology because we're dorks like that.

Whether the situation is good or bad, we can hit a point where we run out of the resources that we need to cope. And that is what *distress* is. *The point of resource depletion.* The point where we need support. It isn't something you can deal with on your own. It isn't a term that identifies someone as tragically fucked up. It's a clinical term that we understand to mean *this person needs some help.*

If you have tipped into distress, maybe it's because life has been throwing you too many curveballs and *then* you also just spilled your coffee and it was the last fucking straw. Or maybe it's a lot of great stuff happening, like you're on a fun trip and you hit exhaustion / sensory overload and the ziplining event reduces you to tears even though you were the one who planned it. They are both distress, not because they're equivalently upsetting but because they're overloading your system.

And it's distress that researchers are talking about when they say that our "stress" numbers are through the roof, *worldwide.* The numbers were bad when I first wrote about them a few years ago, citing Gallup's 2018 Global Emotions Report. Then things got *so much worse.* The American Psychological Association partnered with the Harris Poll in 2022 to see how numbers stood two years into the pandemic. What's up right now? The world is on fire. We have a global pandemic, enormous racial tensions, worries about mass shootings, money problems in general, inflation specifically, and the war in Ukraine. Issues around Covid were reported as stressors, including confusion about mandates and vaccines. But even more importantly, Covid and the ensuing shutdowns drew back the curtain on relationship problems for many people. More than half of the people surveyed reported relationships either ending or becoming incredibly strained during the pandemic.

So clearly, there are a lot of things that can stress us out, many of which have been made much worse by the events of the last few years. Let's look a little more closely at the different types of stressful situations, which account for the issues that we have all been reporting plus some others that are definitely affecting us, though we may not even be considering them as stressors.

Things That Stress Us Out (The Stress Taxonomy)

This is the section where I am supposed to give you examples of possible stressors. And then we all laugh hysterically because there is just so much and we didn't even really scratch the surface. So after doing a deep dive into how other people have written about stress and stressors and categories of stress, I decided to create a taxonomy of sorts instead. I wanted something more useful than a big list. Because if we are talking about something as universal as stress, a very granular list of possible stressors isn't going to be helpful to most of us.

So rather than being hyper-specific about different stressors (and missing tons of important categories in the process) and then getting hyper-specific about what to do about them (e.g., "if you are stressed out by jackhammer noise and you live in an urban area with ongoing construction, buy noise-canceling headphones!"—which may be entirely beyond the point, because the problem is the vibration you feel in your teeth and not the sound in your ears or whatever), I want to focus on how stressors tend to fall into certain categories. Looking at stress categorically may help us later figure out ways to better manage or mitigate it. For example, a stressor over which I have zero-to-little control will often call for a different type of coping skill than a stressor that was created because I didn't manage my boundaries and schedule better, right? OK, so let's look at our super un-official taxonomy.

The Main Categories

These are the larger "is it _____ or _____" categories of potential stressors that help us define our experiences in a more global sense.

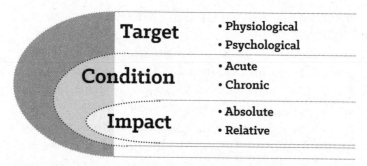

Target
- Physiological
- Psychological

Condition
- Acute
- Chronic

Impact
- Absolute
- Relative

Physiological or Psychological

Physiological stressors are those things that affect the equilibrium of our physical bodies. This could be an injury, health problems, chronic pain, aging and body deterioration, or pregnancy. While these stressors clearly have a psychological impact, they start with something happening to or inside our bodies.

Psychological stressors are the ones that affect the equilibrium of our cognitive-emotional lives. Our thoughts, feelings, and behaviors are filtered through a sense of exhaustion, concern, struggle, or dis-ease. Even those stressors that are wanted and embraced (such as returning to school, getting married, or starting a new job) are adding to our mental load in ways that have some level of negative impact.

Acute or Chronic

Acute stressors are those that are of shorter duration and have a fairly recent onset. Like signing up for a course that is going to last six weeks and noticing that the time, energy, and workload associated with that course are really a lot to manage.

Chronic stressors are those that persist over time or have long-lasting effects. If you are curious about timelines, in the field of medicine, a disease is labeled chronic if it continues for more than three months. I consider this an appropriate timeframe for chronic stressors as well, because the damage we incur in the process of dealing with longer-term stressors can be seen and measured, and this also changes how we approach managing it. Where the acute stressor may be a six-week course, a chronic stressor may be grad school. Yes, there is an end in sight, but it's in the distance to the point of being hazy at the moment, and we need long-term management skills to keep heading in the right direction.

Absolute or Relative

Absolute stressors are those that are universal or near-universal. Meaning anyone in the same situation would have the same response to some degree. And sure, there are always some people who are fine in awful situations, so let's use the rule of thumb created by anthropologist Angeles Arrien here. If 80% of humans would have the same reaction in a particular situation, it's safe to call it universal. Things like pandemic-related stress and the death of a loved one are absolute stressors.

Relative stressors are the ones that are more individualized and are related to our genetics, epigenetics, and unique personal histories. For example, someone who has been deployed and traveled in convoys in war-torn countries will likely find traffic more stressful than a civilian. And a neurodivergent person may find interpersonal interactions more stressful than an allistic person.

The Stressor Subgroups

Here is where we get a little more specific, looking at the impacts of certain situations on our life domains, moral compass, and individual well-being. These categories are not entirely discrete, meaning a stressor you are experiencing may fit into more than one category. But they are, like the above categories, designed to help you think about how to best approach managing a particular stressor. For example, you would likely manage a financial stressor and a relationship stressor in very different ways.

Personal activating stressors are the stressors that are connected to our own personalities/constitutions and events we've experienced. So yes, this is the category that ties specifically to our trauma histories and mental health needs. It is less about a true trauma trigger and more about the uncomfortable associations and reminders of past events that ping our nervous systems in ways that we have to notice and care for. It can also include the stressors that activate our anxiety, our addictions, our unhelpful habits, and other things that aren't directly related to a trauma history but have a strong connection to behaviors that we are working hard to not engage in. For example, having to present at work may activate a panic attack, or being at a party may make you want to drink when you're sober. Managing these situations is stressful because of your history, not because of the event itself.

Snowball stressors are the daily, common disruptions that most everyone faces that have a larger effect over time and/or when we have an extra dose of fuckery. We've all been there: traffic was fucked, our lunch order got messed up, our boss was chingy for no damn reason, a friend was short with us, our partner was grumpy . . . and then a flat tire???? None of these things are pleasant experiences, and all could be considered slightly stressful; but they become more significant when they continue to build up and combine as they roll through our day/week/etc. This also includes the things in our environment that can contribute to sensory overload, like bright lights and loud noises.

Life-balance stressors are the effects of having so much on our schedules that we let our other needs slide. This is the stress caused by not getting enough sleep, not eating things that best nourish and please us, not moving our bodies enough, not having time for pleasure, not attending to our relationships, etc. When the things that make life worth living are eroded in order to make space for the "have-tos," then we start to experience distress.

Significant-life-change stressors are the big life changes that we can't avoid. Sometimes we even seek them out and embrace them, but they still require an outpouring of resources from us. Changing jobs, having kids, getting a partner, getting rid of a partner, experiencing a new illness, and moving are all life-change stressors.

Systems stressors are the stressors related to the organizational systems we all take part in. Work and school are two big ones, but it could also be a group or club you belong to. Or the justice system, should you enter into it. Even positive systems (like the political advocacy group you volunteer for because you believe in it) can cause stress. Being part of a system requires us to contend with the personalities of others (conflict) and follow rules that compromise our sense of agency or autonomy. And most systems also have aspects that don't align with our personal values, which requires us to make choices about how we engage.

Financial stressors . . . because these are huge for almost everyone at some point in their lives, if not for the entirety of their lives. Not having enough money to meet one's needs and/or obligations is such a significant stressor, some researchers have posited that it can lead to traumatic stress and PTSD over time.[7]

Sociorelational stressors are the Jean-Paul Sartre of stressors, since he is the one who famously said "hell is other people." These are the stressors associated with problems or breakdowns in our relationships, as well as loneliness and lack of social supports. We need people, and people can be exasperating, exhausting, disappointing, shady, and generally as people-y as we are. And navigating all that takes energy.

Societal event stressors are stressors that are society-wide if not worldwide. This includes war (and all of the softer synonyms we use for war, like escalating conflict or whatever), environmental issues like climate change, Covid-19, etc.

Knowledge-gap stressors are the stressors associated with not knowing. With being in an unfamiliar situation, which can be concerning and even fear-inducing. These are novel situations where you don't know the rules, like traveling to a new place, starting a new job . . . any scenario where you need to make a decision without access to all available data.

Empathic stressors come from worrying for or about others. This could involve people we know and love, like when you worry about a friend who's going through a significant loss . . . but it can also be generalized to individuals or groups of people that we do not know but that we recognize as experiencing great pain, such

---

7 See my book *Unfuck Your Worth* if you're interested in more on this topic.

as when we know a terrible earthquake has happened in another part of the world and people there do not have food, water, shelter, or safety.

So now that you know all these categories, what are you supposed to do with them in your own life? The idea behind this model is to help you build your own self-awareness so you can strategize and organize your life around your specific needs. I hope you use this list to think about your own responses, patterns, sore points, stuck points, triggers, activators, etc. If you were a client I was seeing in my practice, and you came in frustrated and unhappy and stuck regarding a situation that you were finding incredibly stressful, we wouldn't just focus on strategies to manage it without looking at how it tethers to the whole complex system that is your life, right? It may not change whatever coping strategies we decide would be most effective, but you'd be surprised how often it does.

For example, let's say someone is dealing with chronic illness. Chronic illness has many facets, some of which suck more than others for this individual person. Let's say that I've worked with this person long enough to know that they have a history of having their experiences dismissed, of being called a liar when they spoke of their abuse histories and the like. So upon reflection, we realize that finding a doctor that listens and is affirming and proactive is the part that feels most overwhelming at this particular time. So our coping plan will involve finding a non-shitty doctor, self-coaching around respecting their own truth, and self-advocacy strategies for being seen and heard by the people around them. Your use of this stress taxonomy and the coping strategies later in this book will need to be similarly tailored to your own individual situation and experiences.

CHAPTER 2:
HOW STRESS WORKS IN THE BODY

*O*K, now that we are all on the same page about what constitutes stress and why the world is so damn tired and crabby, let's get even nerdier and dive into the science part. Because while stress is our *response* to situations that are taking time and energy and disrupting our equilibrium . . . that response exists in our bodies, not just in our brains. Like, a lot. So this section is for all my fellow science dorks. I seeeeee you! Those of us who want to understand instead of blindly follow suggestions or prescriptions. I'm not about to ask you to try something until I explain the why. You can skip this part, but you won't because you're also a science dork, right?

The Nervous Systems

Junior high science flashback: Nerves are cells that have special communication functions. Like telephone lines that run all over your body, they communicate as bioelectrical signals. Like, what happens if you touch a hot thing? The nerves in your hand send a message of "FUCKING OW!" to your brain, which then sends a message back saying, "WELL PUT IT THE FUCK DOWN THEN! THAT'S THE LITERAL MEANING OF DROP IT LIKE IT'S HOT!!!"

Our sensory and motor functions are specifically tasked to 12 cranial nerves. Some of these cranial nerves are super specific.

Like the olfactory nerve, unsurprisingly, transmits information about what we smell to our brain. But number 10 of 12, the vagus nerve, is the longest, weirdest, and most complex of the 12 pairs of cranial nerves. The name itself (vagus) comes from the Latin word for "wandering," because this nerve wanders all around the damn body, sending information to organs and tissues. It wouldn't be unreasonable to say that this particular nerve is an information superhighway.

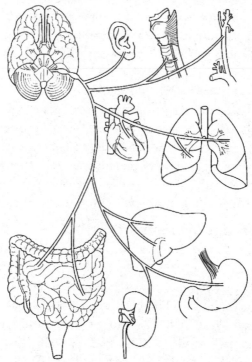

This? The fancy fucking diagram of the vagus nerve. So you can see how the brain communicates with every major organ in your body. No pressure to remain calm then, right?

Nerve cells don't just bop around aimlessly like your useless ex. They are organized into systems. Nervous systems are the networks of the nerve cells and fibers that transmit messages. These systems make the messages transmit more efficiently. So that you will, indeed, drop it like it's hot when need be.

We are going to be focusing a bit on the vagus nerve. Don't worry, this isn't going to be a heavy med-school text. The most important thing to know is that the vagus nerve is the 10th cranial nerve, which connects the brain to all of the internal organs of the body to direct their functioning. Big, important job, right?

Now, while the vagus nerve is the messenger for an entire nervous system, it is only one of several nervous systems that create the entire *human nervous system*. So let's break this down: The human nervous system can be broken up into the central nervous system (brain and spine) and the peripheral nervous system, which connects the brain and spine to the rest of the body. The peripheral nervous system can be split again into two parts:

- The somatic nervous system, which we have voluntary control over

- The autonomic nervous system, which is the part that we do not have voluntary control over and which regulates all of our organs and endeavors to maintain bodily homeostasis

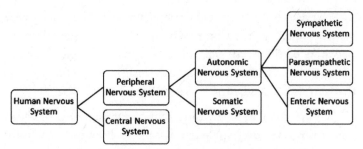

Bodies. So complex and so dumb at the same time. Am I right?

The *autonomic* system is the one we are focusing on in this book. All autonomic means is *self-governing*. These nerves work involuntarily and are not under conscious control. So you are not allowed any time to decide whether or not you are going to drop the hot thing. That's the kind of shit that will get you killed. Your body is not interested in negotiation, shit's just getting dropped. You're starting to feel me on why this is important info, yeah?

The autonomic nervous system has three components: the *sympathetic*, *parasympathetic*, and *enteric* nervous systems. And the vagus nerve is their communication pathway. It's important to understand how they work in relation to each other.

The *sympathetic* nervous system governs our fight-flight-freeze instinct, which is critical to our survival. It is activated in the face of a threat or perceived threat, whether it be to our actual, physical safety, the individuals we love and care for, our possessions, or our needs, wants, desires, well-being, and belief systems. Essentially, anything that challenges the core of who or what we are and who or what belongs to us invokes a protective response. It has nothing to do with how mentally or physically strong we are or how much we love the person or people that we are with. When the sympathetic nervous system kicks in, our ability to be engaged and connected goes offline.

If we perceive aggression as a viable means of staying alive, we will fight. If our instincts tell us we can't fight effectively but we can escape, we will flee. If neither of these responses are likely to be effective, we will freeze.

All of these strategies, even fighting, are purely *defensive* ones. The intent is not to win against or overwhelm the threat, but to survive. The body's job is to size up the situation and figure out the best means of staying alive. It chooses a strategy based on the information it is receiving along with past understanding of the threat. We may move back and forth between strategies as we take in information and gauge our effectiveness at managing the perceived imminent threat. All three responses are part of our defensive survival instincts.

I'm focusing a lot on the freeze response here (official science-y term: dorsal-vagal response) because it's historically been talked about the least, until recently. I am starting to see it show up more often in discussions around dissociation, depersonalization, derealization, and the like. Despite the increased attention, it is still the response that human beings are most embarrassed about, although as a protective strategy, it makes just as much sense as fight and flight do. It's also the most physically dangerous: the freeze response can actually kill you if it goes on too intensely for too long. So why does the body do something so dangerous? Peter Levine (one of the few theorists to talk about the body's survival mechanism and trauma) states that there are four potential evolutionary survival benefits to the freeze response:

- Most predatory animals won't eat an animal they believe is already dead unless they are really hungry. Most animals have encoded information that meat that is already dead may be spoiled and therefore is a risk to eat.

- It is more difficult for predators to detect prey that is not moving. Immobilization shuts down all movement responses. Even if we are trying to be still and quiet it is difficult to do so unless we have become biochemically immobilized.

- When one animal collapses in a group, this distracts the predator from the rest of the group, allowing their escape.

- The freeze response releases a numbing agent in the body that makes the pain of attack more bearable.

Now obviously, it makes sense that the sympathetic nervous system should not be in charge all the time. It would make us fall apart at the seams pretty quickly (and this is why people who don't have conscious ways to cope with chronic stress *do* fall apart at the seams pretty quickly).

Our second nervous system, the *parasympathetic* nervous system, is the one associated with social relationships and bonding. We're pack animals. We need to connect to other human beings for long-term survival, not just for mating season, and navigate the world without feeling batshit crazy and threatened by our surroundings all the time. Being relaxed and alert is how we best engage with the world around us. This means that when the parasympathetic system is in charge, we are able to connect and communicate and form social relationships because we feel safe to do so.

Then comes the researcher that we now associate with polyvagal theory the most, psychologist and neuroscience researcher Stephen Porges. The crux of Porges's research on the vagal system is the finding that our nervous systems work in ranked order (a hierarchy). Safety and connection and relationships—the functions governed by the autonomic nervous systems—rank highest on the hierarchy. But because these processes are managed outside of conscious thought, our ability to remain calm and engaged and relational *is the first thing we lose when our bodies perceive threat.* In order to be our best selves, to live and work in cooperation and build relationships, our bodies have to perceive us as being safe.

And when something challenges our sense of safety at a bodily level, the parasympathetic system goes offline. This works because the sympathetic nervous system is *myelinated,* while the parasympathetic nervous system is not. I know, I know with the science textbook words, but this is actually an important point. Myelination provides insulation, which speeds up the sending of the messages. So the nervous system that is in charge of our stress response works *faster* than the one that is in charge of our chill response.

Both systems operate involuntarily. And the sympathetic nervous system has to be turned off for the parasympathetic nervous system to work, meaning it has to determine that there is no stress or threat and that you are allowed to go about your day. But even when it's not running the show, the sympathetic nervous system is still humming in the background, watching for danger. And it works faster than the chill system, so it will shut shit down at a moment's notice. Any of us with unresolved trauma histories are far more likely to have our parasympathetic systems go offline, putting us into survival mode. We'll get more into this in the next chapter.

The third part of the autonomic nervous system is the *enteric nervous system*, which resides in the gastrointestinal tract. It is the largest of the three autonomic nervous systems, and it has its own unique microcircuits. It receives feedback from the other two systems but is also able to operate independently of them. There are people out there with severed vagus nerves and their enteric nervous systems work just fine. This is some zombie science shit.

The stomach is called the second brain for a reason. Because many neurotransmitters, signaling pathways, and anatomical properties are common to the enteric nervous system and the central nervous system, it's safe to say that the vagus nerve is actually messaging our "gut feelings" to the brain.

Recognizing Your Personal Vagal Responses

OK, so that was a lot of blahblahblah about scienceblahscience. We're about to get into a whole lot of the ways your vagal system can get fucked up, but before we do that, let's start putting this knowledge into practice so you can recognize what's going on in your own body.

But first, there's one more science-y term that you need to know: *vagal tone* just refers to the activity of the vagus nerve—its ability to communicate quickly and effectively. The better its ability to communicate, the healthier we are both physically and mentally. The word "tone" comes from how the effectiveness of vagal communication is measured in terms of heart rate variability, which is interesting (to me) and super-techy and not important to this discussion (for everyone else).

Our body's vagal response has an array of "options." Remember how I said fight, flight, and freeze are all survival responses, and your body is going to read the room and choose the physiological response that makes the most sense? Porges's work visualizes the response options as existing on a ladder, which presumes that we enter and exit certain states in a certain order. I've found this personally confusing and instead use the visualization of a series of flip-switch options rather than a spectrum.

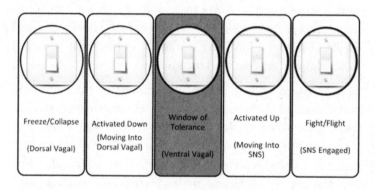

Freeze/Collapse	Activated Down	Window of Tolerance	Activated Up	Fight/Flight
(Dorsal Vagal)	(Moving Into Dorsal Vagal)	(Ventral Vagal)	(Moving Into SNS)	(SNS Engaged)

Imagine a series of light switches, with "safe" in the middle, "too low" on one end, and "too high" on the other, and a couple of switches in between for when you're moving down or up.

Depending on the level of threat detected and previous experiences, the body will flip one switch rather than another, which is why you can go from fight/flight to complete collapse so quickly. The body has to make snap decisions. I have worked with people who only freeze up, others who only fight, and others who run the gamut. Remember how I mentioned earlier that it's about what the body recognizes as its best bet for survival or pain management?

On the "too low" end of the spectrum, you have the freeze/collapse response switch, scientifically known as the dorsal-vagal response. On either end is the sympathetic nervous system switch. On the "too high" end, you've got your fight and flight responses, or as we call it, "SNS Engaged." In the safe center, you have your window of tolerance switch, where your vagus nerve sees no threat and your parasympathetic nervous system is engaged. That's your Baby Bear just-right switch. Like any spectrum, there are shades in between, and you can develop some level of control—you can be activated down into dorsal vagal response or moving up into SNS but then notice that and bring yourself back into your window of tolerance if you need to. That's what we'll be working on here.

Our goal is to stay within our window of tolerance, and learn to expand our window of tolerance as much as possible. In a perfect world, we would become activated enough to deal with potentially threatening situations, but we wouldn't become SNS Engaged or dorsal vagal unless we were under a real attack, right? But a trauma response trains our bodies to presume attack based on the traumas we've experienced. So the threat may not be real in an external sense, but it is very real in our internal world.

The HPA Axis

Stress—or distress—is regulated by something called our "HPA axis," short for *hypothalamic-pituitary-adrenal axis*. This is basically our central nervous system as it is intertwined with our endocrine system, which produces our hormones.

The HPA axis is designed to keep our body balanced (or as scientists put it, in homeostasis). This means, weirdly enough, helping us react appropriately to stress. In order to stay on an even keel, we are meant to deal with problems quickly and efficiently so we can go back to point chill. Two of the main hormones that the HPA axis deploys to deal with stress, however, cause problems when they are activated regularly and run rampant. They are cortisol and adrenaline.

Adrenaline

When our body determines something to be stressful, a cascade of events is set off. The amygdala—the emotional center of the brain—starts the process, sending a signal to the hypothalamus in the brain stem region, which has the task of releasing hormones to help us level up to respond to the stressor. The hypothalamus flips the switch for the sympathetic nervous system to get ready to engage and tells the vagus nerve to shoot a message down to the adrenal glands saying they need to pop the tab on an energy drink.

The adrenal glands say "bet" and release adrenaline into the bloodstream. Adrenaline (also called epinephrine) ups our heart rate and our blood pressure, expands our ability to take more air into our lungs, makes our pupils expand so we can take in more visually, and redistributes blood to our muscles. It gets us ready for action. Adrenaline is our first line of defense. It's such an immediate response that it happens pre-awareness. Whatever we are looking at, hearing, or smelling, we haven't even processed the information in the prefrontal cortex—the thinking brain— but the body is already chugging Red Bull. Because the adrenaline response happens so quickly, it also wears off really quickly. It's that flush of energy you get when you have a really bad scare. Then when you feel kinda nauseous 20 minutes or so later, that's the adrenaline wearing off.

Cortisol

After the adrenaline kicks in, if the amygdala says, "nah, not done yet, need more juice," we end up with cortisol production.[8] Cortisol is also a flip-switch for the sympathetic nervous system, causing rapid heart rate and breathing and all the same energy drink feelings, but for a longer period of time.

Cortisol is slower-acting in the system than adrenaline, since it's the second line of defense and is designed to keep our nervous system on the gas to deal with a longer-lasting situation. It takes more time to build up in the body, and takes longer to dissipate back out. When we are trying to test someone's chronic stress levels, we look at cortisol. Cortisol levels going up are also correlated with vagal tone going down (as measured by heart rate variability), meaning we are far less likely to remain in our window of tolerance.

You've probably heard about how cortisol causes belly fat and heart attacks? That's because it changes the body's metabolism by altering our blood glucose when it is in our system all the damn time. Cortisol also increases amygdala activation and brakes hippocampal activity (which keeps the hippocampus from going in and telling the amygdala to calm its tits), *which leads to more cortisol production* (thanks, brain!).

Continuous cortisol build-up makes our thinking brain (the prefrontal cortex) far less effective. Just like trauma, chronic stress changes the blood flow in the brain because the blood is going to

8 This is where we really see the complexity of the whole system. Cortisol doesn't release on its own. The continued threat signals the hypothalamus to release corticotropin-releasing hormone (CRH), which travels to the pituitary gland (*there's* the P part of HPA!), triggering the release of adrenocorticotropic hormone (ACTH). Then the ACTH runs to the adrenal glands, prompting them to release cortisol. I refrained from putting this in the main text of the book because *ugh* it's a lot of science.

the muscles of the body to prepare us for an attack. Decreased blood flow means decreased brain activity, which creates "holes" in our prefrontal cortex.[9] It fucks with our ability to think clearly and remember things that aren't related to stressful situations. Which is why you feel like you can't think straight when you are really stressed out, because you can't think straight when you are really stressed out.

Cortisol is a total asshole, BTW, if it's something we have in our system on the regular. This whole response in the body makes evolutionary sense. It protected us from predators, right? But that's not modern life, and we are not suited to having this chronic chemical cascade going all the time in the face of everyday stressors.

It's like driving a car and getting stuck in fifth gear. You may still technically be the one driving, but the actual amount of control you have over the car is pretty low. You're kinda just looking for a pile of hay to crash into to avoid as much damage as possible, right? (Hi, yes, I grew up on *The Dukes of Hazzard*, why do you ask?)

---

9 As determined by measuring blood flow and electric activity in the brain through SPECT imaging (single-photon emission computed tomography, if you're nasty).

CHAPTER 3: WHEN STRESS CEASES TO BE MANAGEABLE

S o now we are slightly glassy-eyed from all the science, but we got that down. Which means we are ready to go a little deeper into understanding how stress affects us when it's at its worst. I'm talking about chronic stress, trauma, and survival mode. And because it's your lucky day, this is going to involve a little more science talk.

The Consequences of Chronic Stress

So *how* exactly does a normal, protective stress response lead to chronic, unhealthy distress? There is no single answer, because we are talking about really complex fucking systems. But in the past decade, Western medicine has been catching up to what Eastern medical professionals have been saying for about 3,000 years and functional medicine practitioners have been saying for over a hundred years—that there is quite likely a huge role being played by inflammation.

Inflammation is how the body responds to perceived threats through the production of cytokines activated by the stress response. The cytokines can stay upregulated when stress is chronic, creating the perfect human-body soup in which to cook up some physical and mental health issues.

For one thing, stress is hell on our guts. That chronic production of cortisol is telling the body to get ready to fight, right? And the opposite of the fight/flight response is the rest/digest response. We can see how the body not having time to do the resting/digesting part affects the gut's ability to protect us from other illnesses. The gut does this through an immunoglobulin called secretory IgA. Once that system starts going down, pathogens in the gut start running amuck.

Additionally, all that cortisol starts eating the glutamine (an essential amino acid) in our gut lining, which strips away *another* layer of protection. Then we get gut permeability (meaning pathogens get through the gut lining into the rest of the body). This breaks down our gut lining (and other tissue in our body, such as our muscles), and we are now more likely to have food sensitivities, less able to handle toxin exposures, and more likely to have trouble absorbing nutrients in general.

All of *this* (waves arms around wildly) is modulated by the vagus nerve—both the emotional component and the inflammation component.

Many of the things that can go wrong with us, in terms of physical or mental health, have a stress connection if we perceive them as stressful (more on the perception part and why that can matter later). Naming them all and detailing the connection would be a multivolume book series. WebMD (everyone's favorite internet diagnostic tool) will tell you that chronic stress activates (to name just a couple conditions) heart disease and asthma. And on the "mental" health side, depression and anxiety are strongly correlated with chronic stress.

Physical Symptoms of Chronic Stress

- Cardiovascular issues like abnormal heart rhythms, high blood pressure, heart disease, heart attacks, and strokes

- Disordered eating patterns and weird weight fluctuations due to jacked-up hunger signals from cortisol

- Menstrual problems

- Loss of sexual desire, sexual dysfunction, impotence, and premature ejaculation

- Problems with hair and skin (hair falling out, skin problems like rashes, eczema, acne, etc.)

- Gut upset (IBS, gastritis, ulcers, nausea, GERD, diarrhea, constipation, nausea, etc.)

- Low energy

- Headaches, other aches and pains (chronic or acute), and tension throughout the body

- Racing heart and rapid breathing

- Other nervous behaviors (fidgeting, picking at cuticles, etc.)

- Changes in sleep

- Changes in appetite

- Getting sick more easily than usual (colds, flus, infections)

Emotional/Mental Stuff

- Mental health problems, such as depression, anxiety, PTSD, and thought disorders

- Feelings of agitation and frustration

- Uncontrolled mood swings, racing thoughts

- Thinking you are losing control, being out of control
- Low-level depression; sense of hopelessness, helplessness, or worthlessness
- Inability to relax or enjoy things you usually enjoy
- Avoiding people and situations you generally enjoyed in the past
- Inability to focus, feeling disorganized and forgetful
- Incessant worry
- Making bad choices and judgements
- Always framing things through a negative lens
- Struggling to stay organized and/or focus your attention
- Procrastinating and avoiding responsibilities
- Increased use of substances to manage mood (drugs, alcohol, nicotine, caffeine)

So for those of us with all kinds of continued stress-response upregulation of the HPA axis and its hormonal compadres, we start seeing the effects in our lives. It can also be complicated, because many of the symptoms of stress can be symptoms of other things. Is it stress or is it *immediate-death butt cancer*?

Saying this loud and clear for the people who are worried about going all woo-woo and ignoring other serious medical issues: We always need to rule out other medical stuff that might be going on. And even if it isn't immediate-death butt cancer, it's still serious. Your body is trying to get your attention. Because early stress symptoms turn into chronic problems within the body, which can lead to serious illness (and yes, more on that later).

Additionally, you may have already had some of these issues and then they got exacerbated by stress. Everyone with a chronic physical or mental illness is totally nodding their head right now. When you look back at all of the chemicals associated with the stress response and look at how they operate within the body, this list starts to make tons of sense.

Stress affects everyone differently. And clearly, the more chronic the stress, the more likely it is to cause a cascade of issues. Which brings us to . . .

When Chronic Stress Becomes Worse (General Adaptation Syndrome)

When chronic stress starts to cause more severe issues, we have what's long been referred to as *adrenal fatigue*. Except you won't find that diagnosis on your medical records anywhere. The problem is although it sounds clinical as fuck, adrenal fatigue still isn't an accepted medical diagnosis. Adrenal insufficiency can be measured on lab work, while adrenal fatigue cannot.

Whether we call it adrenal fatigue, general adaptation syndrome, or hypoadrenia, there is no real diagnostic criteria to determine it exists. It's a catchall term for a set of symptoms like body aches, fatigue, nervousness, sleep disturbances, and digestive problems. It's hard to define what we can't measure. And the medical establishment understandably worries that there is another medical illness causing those symptoms that is being left untreated, like major depression, Addison's disease, or even myalgic encephalomyelitis.

And that's entirely fucking fair. Again, other serious medical issues should always be ruled out first. But if we do rule out other stuff and are still feeling low-level shitty all the time, we should consider that our bodies are not designed for being in a constant state of stress. Modern living and anticipatory distress have made it far more likely that we remain in this state of disequilibrium on an ongoing basis. And with more and more research linking patterns of adrenal hormone output to other chronic illnesses, I think that we are doing ourselves a disservice by dismissing that the cascade of events caused by the stress response, if activated constantly, causes dysregulation of the HPA axis. One term I've seen more recently in response to this idea is *HPA-D* (HPA dysregulation) as a replacement for adrenal fatigue.

So rather than looking just at adrenal output as a measure of disease, we are looking at the entire system becoming hypo-activated. That is, slowing down from overuse.[10] It's the body's way of adapting physiologically to the constant influx of stress hormones—by decreasing production of those same stress hormones. Just like the whole of HPA axis activation is a complicated process, so is the adaptation of the process to chronic stress, which appears as HPA dysregulation. And when we slow down on producing stress hormones, our body is less able to effectively respond to stress (which remains a legitimate need), which causes more stress, and begins the cycle again. This can lead to more complex physical and mental health issues, like . . .

While we can't measure issues within the adrenal glands until they are shutting down (which then gives us a possible diagnosis of a disease like Addison's, Cushing's, etc.), we can measure for patterns of elevated cortisol with a fairly simple saliva test. We can also measure an individual's cortisol awakening response and their cortisol-to-DHEA ratio.

---

10 I have a middle-aged body and I resemble this.

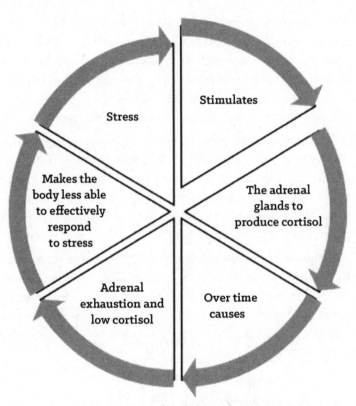

How we think HPA-D continues to self-reinforce

Even easier than that? Another common symptom of HPA dysregulation is orthostatic postural hypotension. Meaning, a drop in blood pressure when you stand up. If I suspect HPA-D, I will have someone lie down on the floor and take their blood pressure after resting there for a few minutes (the floor in my office is clean, though, it's cool). Then I will have them stand up and take it again. Normally, someone's blood pressure should go up when they stand up, but if it drops (especially by 10 or more points), that's a sign of HPA-D. The bigger the drop, the bigger the problem is likely to be. I know this sounds a little redonkulous, but a recent study of patients in Poland found orthostatic hypotension in all of the study participants who had both adrenal insufficiency and adrenal crisis (which occurs when a lack of sufficient cortisol creates a medical emergency).

Long story short, there are usable testing techniques that we can employ to recognize a body overloaded by stress before we develop an even more complex and chronic mental health issue. I see it as akin to treating chronic allergies before they become a bronchial infection or pneumonia. We can also look at good old clusters of symptoms in our lives.

The symptoms associated with HPA-D may feel super vague to you, but they are still a good starting point. And when we see certain patterns in symptoms we can get a better idea of what's going on. Symptoms of HPA-D due to chronic stress can look somewhat different from stress symptomatology. Here's what we look for:

- Difficulty getting up in the morning

- High levels of fatigue each day

- Inability to handle stress (small things get really big, really fast)

- Cravings for salty foods

- Higher energy levels in the evenings (and not just because you are finally away from your stupid job or school day)

- Overuse of stimulants like caffeine (I feel attacked)

- A weak immune system (every bug that makes the rounds, you get)

If this sounds super familiar to you, it's another case where it's good to find a doctor who takes this stuff seriously. Not one who says, "Hahaha, just relax, it's not that bad!" Making lifestyle changes is hard work, but you're already doing the hard work of living with an exhausted body, so this will be a cakewalk in comparison!

Stress and Trauma

Whenever we talk about how stress works in the body, we need to talk about trauma. A trauma is an event that happens outside our understanding of how the world is supposed to work. A trauma response is when our ability to cope with what happened goes to shit and it's affecting other areas of our life.

There are lots of things that can operate as a trauma. And in most of my books we are looking specifically at the kinds of injuries that we recognize as leading to a diagnosis like PTSD. But as I have also talked about in those books, there are plenty of things that are deeply traumatic for many people but aren't really considered by our diagnostic manuals. These injuries are nearly universal and often are not even thought of as traumatic events because of their universality. Gabor Maté refers to them as "little-t traumas," meaning they maybe don't register diagnostically (really nice way of saying they aren't considered bad enough to merit a diagnosis within the DSM) but still cause harm to our psyches.

A trauma can be an accident, an injury, a serious illness, a loss . . . or any kind of life event that kicks your ass, even if you manage to push it aside at the time. We can call it a nervous system injury. Or an acquired brain injury. Or any number of things, and all of them would be true. It can include hurtful and impactful injuries that happen so regularly that we don't even maintain a conscious awareness of them, and definitely aren't considering how they may impact us in the future.

No matter whether they're big-T or little-t traumas, they all pile up and serve to deplete us, fracture our psyches, and cause both intra- and interpersonal problems. A trauma response is what happens inside us in response to what happens to us whenever we do not have time and space to heal.

How Our Brains Handle Trauma

Most of the time, it takes about three months to reestablish equilibrium after a trauma. That is, after about 90 days, our emotional sensors are no longer operating in hyper-warp-speed mode, and they return to normal.

Using the word *normal* is total bullshit, of course. Of course, it's not really normal, no matter how well you recover. Traumas change us forever. So this so-called normal is more of a *new normal*. We find a way to live and cope with the situation that happened, the loss of what the world used to be, and an acceptance of what it is now. We still experience feelings surrounding whatever happened—feelings that may never completely go away. But our amygdala isn't super haywire over the situation after a few months. Hijack mode deactivated.

But approximately a third of the time, after a trauma, we don't recover to a new normal. We have a trauma response instead, based on our experience of *traumatic stress*.

Once you start operating from a trauma-informed experience (whether full-blown PTSD or not), you can see signs of the following in your life as the brain tries to manage your trauma with adaptive strategies. Which is just a grad-school-word way of saying we create great ways to avoid our trauma responses so we don't have to deal with them. But it's a foundation that was built on unsteady ground. Cracks start to develop.

- **Arousal:** The amygdala is always wearing its crazy pants, and you find yourself freaked out when you shouldn't be or don't want to be. You may or may not know why. But your brain may process something it considers a threat that you aren't even cognizant of, and all of a sudden you are falling apart in the middle of the grocery store.

- **Avoidance:** You find yourself avoiding things that trigger arousal. Grocery store was bad? I can order my groceries online. Really don't need to leave the house for groceries, right?

- **Intrusion:** Thoughts, images, memories related to the trauma experience start shoving their way up. The things that your brain was protecting you from don't actually go away, and they start bubbling to the surface without your consent. This isn't the same as rumination, where you worry over a bad memory intentionally; it's where stuff shows up when least expected. And you can't manage everything that is bubbling up.

- **Negative Thoughts and Feelings:** With all this other stuff going on, is it any wonder that you never feel good? Or even just OK?

These are the essential four horsemen of the PTSD apocalypse. It's how we diagnose full-blown PTSD. When they're present, it means that at some level you are reliving your trauma in your head at any given moment.

But not everyone having a trauma response has full-blown PTSD. A PTSD diagnosis is a checklist, in the end. Someone who is evaluating you for this diagnosis will be looking to see if you have a given number of these symptoms. So some people meet some of the criteria for PTSD, but not enough to warrant a diagnosis.

But not meeting all the criteria for PTSD does not put you in the all-clear or make you magically feel any better, right? You are clearly not OK now, and there is a pretty damn good chance that it is gonna get worse.

The VA figured this out when studying 9/11 first responders. Of the people who had some symptoms of a trauma response but not full-blown PTSD, 20% showed a symptom increase that qualified them for a PTSD diagnosis two years later when they were reassessed. *Go fucking figure* that if you keep reliving your trauma, those connections keep reinforcing in your brain.

Thoughts, feelings, and behaviors that are driven by our trauma response can be really difficult things to understand. Not just for the people around us, but even for ourselves. Have you ever had a moment like that? When you were thinking, "What the actual FUCK, brain?" We feel clueless and the people who love us feel helpless.

But let's give our dick-for-skittles brain a break here. It's the brain trying to make sense of shit. Shit that may not actually make sense in reality. So it goes all over-reactive in how it demands you respond to certain events. And those certain memories trigger negative emotions. And the brain reacts in a protective way without you even realizing what's going on.

One of the things Gabor Maté did brilliantly in his book *The Myth of Normal* was go through some of the research on the more subtle ways that unhealed trauma shows up in our lives.

Since these are less obvious than the hallmarks of PTSD I just reviewed, they are often equated with little-t traumatic events. Many people don't realize that they are responding from a brain that has been re-coded for safety by the impacts of all of these events. These subtle manifestations of trauma include the following:

- **Limited response flexibility** refers to our diminished capacity to think through our responses. To recognize that our first impulse may not be the most skillful choice. Response flexibility is something we develop as we get older. Babies don't have it, right? They learn it. The part of the brain most engaged is the mid-frontal part of the cerebral cortex, which we know develops through at least our mid-20s. The significance of the traumatic events, how many you experienced, and how young you were when you experienced them all play a role in diminishing your response flexibility. And stress? All kinds of stress, not just traumatic stress, activates these rigid response patterns.

- **Altered worldview** refers to how we become more invested in a singular outlook on life and have a harder time seeing the complexity of the world and the situations we encounter. We typically have a darkened worldview, meaning we see and experience the world as only negative, scary, and unjust. But an altered worldview can also produce newly minted members of the Love and Light Brigade. Meaning, the people who spiritually bypass the complexity of existence by deciding everything is just fine and dandy. If either side of this sounds like extremist politics to you? I'm with ya on that—same team.

- **Loss of present-focus** refers to how we become disconnected from ourselves based on the fucked-up things that have happened to us. As Dr. Maté explains, this leads to us being more easily attacked by all the influences that reinforce our trauma and exploit our personhood.

There are other subtle changes that many people may experience around traumatic, toxic stress. So before we go into tools for management, it's important that we talk about some of these other less obvious and therefore more insidious responses. These are issues that we have seen inundate our media feeds and news cycles without much explanation as to what they really mean. So let's dig into (just a little, and no final exam after, pinky swear) the formation and impact of living in survival mode.

Survival Mode: An Exhausted Brain Just Trying to Survive

The concept of "survival mode" is one that clinicians use a lot, though it is not an official, DSM-y linguistic choice. Like the term "flashbacks," which originally described a filmmaking technique for telling stories about a character's past, survival mode is also a media-related term that we've adapted to other uses. In video games, survival mode is when we have to continue playing without dying in a pause-free game for as long as we can while the game itself gets faster and more difficult. Also, no additional support is provided in the process.

So let's talk about what clinicians mean when we say someone is living in survival mode. The short version is life has been so exhausting and so overwhelming for so long that their focus is on surviving, not thriving. This can be related to trauma but can also be caused by stress, grief, or any other sustained difficult emotion or situation. People living in poverty (and I mean POOR, not temporarily BROKE) often live in survival mode. It means we are existing moment to moment and struggle to consider anything beyond the short term.

What's going on in survival mode? Our prefrontal cortex, the newest part of the human brain, is the thinking brain. It's where our executive function skills reside. These are things like planning for the future, thinking through options critically, and being able to organize and problem solve. Being able to best manage our emotions without getting the fallout from them. When we are our best selves, we are able to deliberate, consider, weigh options, and make choices grounded in all possible considerations.

I've written (ad nauseam, sorry) about how trauma affects the prefrontal cortex (in my book *Unfuck Your Brain* and every other book that has my name on it for time eternal). The term "trigger," clinically, refers to the experience of reliving a past traumatic event in the present. You're walking through the store, for example, and someone in there sounds just like your abusive father and suddenly you're eight years old again, ducking for cover. Your amygdala takes over.

Why? Because those older parts of the brain are not only designed for protection over reason, they also work faster than the prefrontal cortex. Executive function skills require time, consideration, and discernment. And if your brain gets activated to danger, it's going to go into protective mode. We do not have time for the slower process of consideration. Staying alive means erring on the side of caution, every time.

So when clinicians are referring to survival mode, we are looking at very similar processes. We don't mean someone who is currently triggered or re-experiencing an unhealed trauma. Rather, we're talking about someone who has struggled for so long to just make it through life that their executive function processes have become dimmed by the sheer volume of awful things they have to manage, the utter lack of support and care, and the paucity of healthy choices and resources. Where someone with PTSD may be triggered and react in a way that's conducive to immediate escape, someone living in survival mode may be able to be somewhat future focused, but not in the long term. Their decision-making processes have become so worn thin that what may be clear to everyone around them isn't at all discernable to them in their current state. Think of trauma reactivity as turning off the prefrontal cortex completely and survival mode as a prefrontal cortex dimmer switch.

Survival mode can look like the following:

- **Fatigue/Low Energy:** This means feeling depleted even if you get a good amount of rest (and even more fun if you haven't). The depletion may be physical, emotional, or even spiritual.

- **Depleted Self-Care:** Less or no self-care, either intentionally ("I don't have time or space for this") or unintentionally (simply forgetting). It means not eating foods that are healthy and nourishing (or eating on the run or not eating at all), not taking care of our hygiene, not maintaining a sleep schedule, not moving our bodies.

- **Being Focused Only on the Present or Immediate Future:** This means we are only handling the day-to-day, maybe a few days out but not much past that. If we keep our heads down to stay in the grind, there isn't much time to look at what might be possible a year out if we start working toward it now.

- **Emotional Lability:** Meaning feeling anger, overwhelm, sadness, or other emotions far more easily than we have in the past. Which can lead to feeling activated or breaking down far more frequently.

- **Isolation:** This could be because we are operating on autopilot and not even thinking about connecting with others. It could also be because of the exhaustion or our concern over our emotional lability. The isolation can be conscious or unconscious.

- **Increased Impulsivity:** This can be related to being more shortsighted, but can also exist on its own. Even if you recognize the longer-term consequences, the need to feel better in the moment takes precedence. You may use more substances, spend more money, engage in activities that don't serve you well, or engage in activities to excess.

Why does all of this matter to a conversation about stress? Like in the conversation about little-t traumas above, we are looking at the more subtle ways that long-term distress causes us to experience a diminishment of everything that makes us human and makes it worth being alive. In survival mode, we are less skillful in the face of struggle and we are less joyful about the things that make life worth living. We hear terms like "burnout" and "survival mode" all over the damn place, and they are incredibly important concepts (stay tuned for a discussion of burnout in chapter 8). But they are often presented in bite-sized social media engagement pieces where we lose the deeper connection to what is happening to us and why. Which makes our own healing harder to accomplish, which makes us feel even more like failures. And if we are going to put all this work into our own healing, we need as much information as possible. Because there are no one-size-fits-all solutions, and we have to understand ourselves and all of the cultural systems around us to have a fighting chance.

Can Stress Be Diagnosed?

The DSM (current edition is the DSM-5-TR) does have a section titled "Trauma- and Stressor-Related Disorders," so the short answer is you can have stress diagnosed—kinda. All of the diagnoses in this category are related to the direct experience or witnessessing of a traumatic event. Everyday stressors, no matter how bad and fucked up, do not count in DSM Land.

We've already gone over PTSD. The other possible diagnosis for an adult is acute stress disorder . . . but what it refers to is a more recent traumatic event and our response to it. If someone had something fucked up happen to them and they are still in the three-days-to-one-month window after it happened? Acute stress disorder is the diagnostic code we assign to say "this human being is going to develop PTSD if we don't fucking help them right fucking now."

The other diagnoses in this chapter of the DSM-5-TR relate to children and include reactive attachment disorder (which is more internalized and looks an awful lot like a depressive disorder) and disinhibited social engagement disorder (which, as the name suggests, is more about externalized and risky behaviors).

So if you are wanting to go to therapy for your non-trauma-related stress (whether acute or chronic) and want insurance to actually pay for it? You and your therapist will have to look at other options. Adjustment disorders are the most common diagnostic choice, since they operate as a bit of a catchall category for any changes in mood or behavior in reaction to events in our lives. They can be noted as including depressive symptoms, anxiety symptoms, conduct issues (meaning being shitty or destructive or otherwise acting a fool), or any combination thereof. Additionally, if the symptoms are more than mild, a clinician qualified to provide a diagnosis may also consider a mood disorder, an anxiety disorder, a dissociative disorder, and the like.

I know, I know. You're thinking *"OK, but?"* and I feel you. There are plenty of circumstances that are stressful enough to bring on a trauma response. I've worked there too, gone to school there too, and had that relationship too. There are two catchall categories in the DSM section mentioned above that may fit if you're experiencing a stress-related trauma response that doesn't fit the criteria for PTSD. The first is called "other specified trauma- and stressor-related disorder" and the second is called "unspecified trauma- and stressor-related disorder."

The "other specified" category relates to when the stress or trauma reactions are causing impairment but in ways that don't match the standards of a more specific diagnosis. In this case the clinician does document what kinds of reactions the person is having. Like, a level of distress that is more significant than a standard adjustment disorder but isn't full-blown PTSD. Or it's related to complex bereavement. Or even culture-bound syndromes like *ataque de nervios* (which is defined more broadly than anxiety or a panic disorder).

The "unspecified" category is the one used when the clinician is not delineating the underlying issues for any number of reasons. It could be because no one actually knows. Or (and this is the reason that I am bringing it up) the clinician making the diagnostic impression (along with the person they are diagnosing) is choosing not to specify why the criteria for PTSD or acute stress disorder were not met. This is a diagnosis code that gives you the option of pointing out that someone is dealing with pretty significant trauma and stress, is struggling in different areas of their life, and is living in survival mode. Maybe the issues they are facing do not meet the narrow definitions of traumatic stress as defined by the DSM, but their pain is real and the impact is real.

Part Two:
Coping with
Stress

So that was a lot of science and a lot of heavy stuff about trauma. But no matter what kind of stress we're talking about, the reality is that most of us don't choose stress, we just have to deal with it. Whether it's everyday stress, life-events stress, traumatic stress, or disintegration-of-society stress, this is the shitshow we've been handed. And research shows the more we try to avoid stress, the worse it gets. So what does help?

That's what this next part of the book is for. Now that we know all about what stress is and how it can wreak havoc on our minds and bodies, we're going to figure out how to deal with it. We're going to go over all kinds of coping skills, from in-the-moment survival strategies to longer-term ways to transform your relationship with stress (and maybe even your relationships with other people, for good measure).

CHAPTER 4:
THE BASICS OF COPING

We are all cursed with living in interesting times. Even when shit is rocking along and our lives are generally positive, we are not fucking likely to focus on calmness or give ourselves space to think and chill. Remember when vacation was meant to be a time to have fun adventures? Now it's a time to go away and sit somewhere and be as quiet, non-thinky, and non-doey as possible. I work with so many people who just need more time in their lives to chill. They aren't crazy, they are just fucking stressed out and *exhausted*.

We are all seeking better ways to live with all this shit, right? When I say "all this shit" I am talking about what it means to be human in the 21st century. We are living in a time of huge uncertainty. Political upheaval, community violence, environmental distress. We are hyper-wired and overstimulated. And undernourished in all the ways that matter: authentic connection, stillness, healthy nourishment, joyful movement. We are seeking relief even more desperately than Aidan Quinn was seeking Susan.

Let's look at what's gotten super popular in recent years. Pokémon Go. Fidget spinners. Coloring, having house plants, baking bread. These are all things that help soothe our minds when life is a dumpster fire. And there will likely be at least three more viral coping skill activities sweeping Insta between now and when this book is published. We NEED shit to help manage life stress. These are all *coping skills activities*. We are all actively seeking ways to manage things that feel unmanageable.

Remember that 2022 stress survey I talked about in Chapter 1, by the American Psychological Association and the Harris Poll? That same study also showed that our tools for coping with stress are stretched thin. About half of the people surveyed reported using prayer as a tool when faced with stress or challenge, and about the same number of people reported that they handled stress or challenge by "just enduring it." About 30% of people reported upping their comfort food intake when stressed, and millennials and Gen Z reported they were more than twice as likely to take a stress nap than to work out when stressed.

And this is not a disparagement of comfort food or naps. I am a big fan of both, as sometimes nothing hits better than some fast food mashed potatoes when my head is pounding and I've hit Code Overwhelm. I present these numbers not to shame people for doing whatever they can to manage their load, but to demonstrate that everything we are coping with is functionally exhausting and we feel stuck and powerless so often that considering other tools and options seems impossible.

So before we talk about specific types of coping skills and how they work and all that therapist-y bullshit, I want to say a few things as clearly as possible and as *loudly* as possible for those of y'all hovering around in the back. *Needing coping skills is not a sign of weakness or mental illness.* It means you are a normal human being navigating a truly abnormal culture. Lily Tomlin once said, *"Reality is the leading cause of stress amongst those in touch with it."*

There are a few things that are complete and fundamental truths about you and why you sometimes are struggling and need coping skills:

- There are no such things as wrong responses, only adaptive ones.

- What you have survived has wired your body to proceed with extreme caution on an unconscious level at all times. This is called staying fucking alive and safe.

- You are not choosing to shut down.

- This is not a "mental" illness, it is a physiological state of the human body.

- You are not crazy, you have adapted to the environment around you with the only information you had at the time . . . your previous circumstances.

You may be thinking, "Bitch, stop being overly nice and letting me off the hook. I'm just fucking crazy and I don't need an apologist right now."

Yeah, here's the thing. I'm not nice. Empathic? Definitely. But nice and letting people off the hook? Never been accused of that in the history of ever. You are absolutely accountable for your actions, no matter what bullshit has been foisted upon you. You may not have been the one who bought the ticket, but it is now officially both your circus and your monkey.

Words change in meaning over time and across situations. Sometimes words become so vaguely all-encompassing that we lose a common understanding of their meaning. And if our job here is to figure out how to use coping skills to get better, we need to start with a common understanding of meaning.

"Coping skills" is one of those phrases that we use all the time and have a general idea of what it means, but maybe couldn't define coherently if pressed to do so. For our purposes, I'm going to define it as:

> A *conscious* effort to utilize resources to manage or mitigate stressors. The stressors are either internal (in the form of health issues, trauma flashbacks, negative self-talk wiring, etc.) or external (bad shit happening, other people's drama, all the crazy shit going on in the world, etc.).

Coping skills are the tools we use to manage stress and prevent a freefall into distress. They also help us negotiate with our triggers and mitigate our response if we are triggered.

Y'all are with me, right?

Of course, you can totally argue a broader definition here. Coping skills can be *any* way we react to our interpersonal and intrapersonal conflict to self-soothe, conscious or not. The Freuds (both Sigmund and Anna) called these sorts of unconscious coping strategies *defense mechanisms*. More recently, Jungian analyst James Hollis referred to them as *reflexive anxiety management systems*.

But we need to frame coping skills in a more conscious and proactive way. The history of mental health treatment is replete with warnings that if we don't cope with stressors consciously and productively, our brains will create coping skills for us. And they won't be healthy. For example, left to its own devices my brain is a fan of nachos and bed rotting.

When dealing with the physiological and psychological impact of stress, the body's main task is to return to equilibrium.

Which means it is using whatever tools are at its disposal. This isn't maladaptive, it's smart. Because we *need* coping skills. We need resources to combat stress and prevent distress. And we need mechanisms to manage our reactions to being triggered. When you learn new tools and start making new neural pathways around using them, it will get easier and easier to do so.

So the second part of this book is focused on conscious and proactive coping. As you've probably gathered from Part One, we have a pretty good understanding of the brain and how it works, and that understanding is getting better all the time. We know that brains are just looking to survive. But in the end, we are so much more than embodied brains, sending and receiving messages. That *undefinable more-ness* that makes us our unique selves is the human mind. And you need more than just your brain: it takes the human mind to thrive and heal.

That's why this next part of the book is about being MIND-focused instead of BRAIN-focused. It's centered on how we use coping skills to take our power back in incredibly demanding, frustrating situations. Because, seriously. What the actual literal FUCK is happening in the world right now???? Sometimes the only power we have is in our own reactions. And if that is the only damn thing we have left, let's hold on as tight as possible to our sanity and humanity.

And, hey. Another note. What about all the stupid shit that gets under our skin? Going back to our definitions of stress and distress, it's not actually stupid. If something requires our resources, big or small, then it just does. And if we are low on resources, spilling our Americano (the adult equivalent of letting go of your balloon, dontcha know) can be as distressing as a car accident. Maybe not physically or behaviorally, but emotionally. You feel me?

Sidenote for Therapists and Other Treatment Providers: I'm sure you are wondering where I am going with all this and if it will work with the theoretical orientation you operate from. Yo, I hope so! I've intentionally pulled what I have found to be the best and most effective resources from a variety of evidence-based practices and well-established treatment theories. You are gonna find your cognitive behavioral therapy, dialectical behavioral therapy, acceptance and commitment therapy, positive psychology, mindfulness-based stress reduction, somatic experiencing, relational-cultural therapy, and classic Jungian therapy. Eclecticism at its best!

Common Challenges to Coping

Coping skills are not woo-woo bullshit. They are mechanisms for managing an altered physiological state and bringing your parasympathetic nervous system back online. They are ways of thinking, feeling, and behaving through a physical state of stress. We cannot control our brain's survival responses, but we can negotiate with them to demonstrate that their situational read is not accurate and that we can manage our current circumstances.

But coping skills are complicated because we have these unique human minds that interact with these self-preserving human brains. And we are really good at thinking too much about something or not thinking nearly enough before we act. Essentially, we are super good at getting ourselves in trouble in the following ways:

- We have coping skills but they are unhealthy.

- We *had* coping skills but they've stopped working.

- We don't have enough strategies to fall back on when the skills that usually work don't work.

- We forget to use our strategies in the moment.

- We aren't sure which strategies we should use in which situations.

So how do we resolve these issues and be better at this coping shit?

- *Lots* of fucking practice—when you aren't activated. The therapeutic term for this is "over-learning." Don't practice until you get it right, practice until you are incapable of getting it wrong. As Bruce Lee said, *"Under duress, we do not rise to our expectations, but fall to our level of training."*

- Trying out *lots* of different options. If you have a couple skills that typically work for you, that's awesome. You will be far more successful if you have several more good skills in your back pocket in case your brain goes into asshole mode and doesn't respond to your tried-and-true strategies.

- Code what you are dealing with. I've created four categories of coping skills (more on that in the next section). Two are emotion-focused (meaning they are designed to deal with our internal response to something that has to be lived through, not changed) and two are problem-focused (meaning they are designed to help you navigate the world in a different way to overcome whatever bullshit you are currently having to cope with). Those aren't finite categories. Because you have to manage your own response before you go out to change the world. But being able to identify whether or not a problem-focused coping skill is warranted at any point may help stop you from doing something unproductive. Like trying to forcibly change an unchangeable situation and being frustrated with your lack of success, when your energy would have been better spent learning to manage your own internal reactions to the bullshit around you and being really successful at those emotion-focused coping skills.

Types of Coping Skills

There are eleventy billion ways to define and categorize coping skills. Or at least, it felt that way when I was reading up on them. None of these ways of conceptualizing coping quite fit how *I* view the coping process, however, so I decided to create my own framework (much like how I decided to create my own stress taxonomy . . . I sure like to make life difficult for myself, don't I?).

Why was I so determined to do that and why are you going to see a category list that didn't exist until it fell into place in my brain while driving to work one morning? Many of the coping skills categories that other writers and theorists have created separate out cognitive coping skills from emotional coping skills. That's hardly useful when they both inform each other in a continuous feedback loop.

We are feeling beings more than we are thinking beings. We feel first, and that informs our thoughts. Some counseling theories state that you can absolutely never separate the two at all, even going so far as to refer to them as one entity: *feeling-thoughts*. So any coping skills worth a shit are going to target both the thought and the feeling.

Other categorizations that make me cranky include separating coping skills into categories like "helpful" and "unhelpful." Very few coping skills exist in a finite dichotomy of good or bad, so it would be bullshit for me to pretend otherwise while operating as the decider. Other categorizations I found in the literature tended to be more limited in scope, like focusing on an individual's ability to engage in a job that helps them feel they are having a positive impact in the world. Occupation as its own coping skill category? As we so eloquently say at my house, *fucking really?* Having that kind of job is a rare privilege (I know because I DO have that kind of job), and most of us have to find other ways to feel we are making a positive impact on the world around us.

So here is the breakdown I came up with, based on how the brain works (because, science) coupled with the fact that reality is quite often a dumpster fire (because, society). The presumption that we all have the luxury of being proactive world-changers is cruel, and insisting otherwise becomes a mechanism for mind-fucking people into thinking they are complete failures at managing the human condition. So I created my coping skill categories based on how the world actually works.

Live Through This **Skills:** These are for when the shit hits the fan and the only power you have lies in your own response. It's survival-without-losing-your-damn-mind time.

Internal Judo **Skills:** Here is where we get a bit deeper and change our relationship with the bullshit in our own minds. How do we make space with what's going on in our minds to give ourselves more of a sense of control, but without blowing smoke up our own asses?

Mitigate the Bullshit **Skills:** This is where we get more behavior-oriented. How can we structure what we do to create better outcomes in response to the craziness around us?

Finding the Pony **Skills:** These are the society-changing, expert-level coping skills that can be used to make the world a better place without actual world domination. The secret bonus part is that it's stuff that makes the other stuff easier to do as well, so you get to be a living saint *and* selfish as fuck at the same time.

Organizing the coping skills in this way may help you process whatever kind of stressor you are facing (see the stress taxonomy from earlier in the book) through different types of skills. For example, maybe the *live through this* skills will be more effective when you're going through something chronic and universal. But I don't want to flowchart how the stressors line up with the skills, because everyone is different. Let's look at that situation: going through something chronic and universal, such as living in a country at war. Maybe *live through this* skills work best, but maybe *mitigate the bullshit* skills better fit how you see the world and what kind of response is most empowering to you. There is no right answer, except figuring out how to best care for yourself in barely tenable situations.

Basic Coping, Navy SEAL Style

Before getting deep into those four categories of coping skills (which we'll do in the upcoming chapters), I thought it would be helpful to start with an introductory set of coping skills that are potentially usable by everyone. Easy-peasy, right? Then it really took me a while to come up with something truly all-encompassing. Until I remembered the Navy SEALs. And how does one, for even one minute, forget the Navy SEALs, FFS?

Backstory time. The Navy works hard to select the most badass, physically fit specimens of humanity for SEAL training. First these recruits have a bunch of "developmental" courses they have to navigate. Then comes the infamous six-month Basic Underwater Demolition/SEAL training (BUD/S) course.

Despite the Navy's expertise in selecting candidates that are physically up to the task, the dropout rate for individuals attending SEAL school is really damn high (like 75% high). After years of this, the Navy commissioned psychologists to figure out what was different about the 25% that succeeded. And they found, unsurprisingly, that it was a form of mental ability, not physical ability. There were four essential abilities that were later termed "The Four Pillars of Mental Toughness," and the ideas within them really encompass all the coping skill categories that I listed above. The four pillars represent a seriously well-woven set of coping skills we can all learn from.

Pillar One: Very Short-Term and Very Specific Goal Setting

Goals that are going to take a while or are sort of nebulous are recipes for disaster. We need a quantifiable endpoint and we need to see it right up ahead. Navy SEALs who focused on getting through the training activity at hand rather than the course overall were far more successful in finishing the entire program. "OK, let me get through this assignment, I can always quit after," is literally how I talked myself through my doctoral program, y'all.

Pillar Two: Positive Mental Visualization

This means mentally watching yourself successfully complete the task you set out to accomplish or endure the bullshit you need to endure. We are wired for the negative as a species survival skill, which means we visualize failure, which leads to the brain saying ABORT MISSION. We can replace that automatic response with a positive walk-through and a successful outcome. And we are far more likely to achieve that outcome if we do.

Pillar Three: Positive Self-Talk

Check this shit out: Our rate of inner dialogue is far higher than our capacity for verbal speech. It's actually been clocked at 4,000 words a minute! And again, since we are wired for the negative, we tend to speechify negative ideas. Instead, if we intentionally use positive self-talk, mantras, and encouragement, we are far more likely to succeed. Remind yourself this ain't no thang compared to everything else you've been through. And hell, your survival rate thus far is 100% so the odds are in your favor, rock star.

Pillar Four: Managing Self-Arousal

Managing our cortisol and adrenaline production is a huge part of coping in general. Techniques that keep the body calm in turn keep the feeling-thoughts better managed. Breathing techniques are a big part of that, which is why I include different variations of them in so much of what I write. One of the basic ones that SEALs use is a simple 4x4 technique. In for four, then out for four. It's less complicated than some of the others, which makes it easier to use when your brain and body are going into absolute panic mode (such as when, during BUD/S training, candidates have their wrists and ankles tied before they are dumped into a pool to simulate drowning and the breathing part doesn't work so good anymore). Breathing techniques can help us so much in immediate moments of utter terror. Because it is such good medicine for many circumstances, a slightly more enhanced version of SEAL breathing is included as one of my favorite *live through this* skills in the next chapter.

OK, awesome. Now that we can invoke some SEAL-ing as appropriate, how about some more basic coping skills that can be helpful to pretty much anyone? Got you on those, too!

Gratitude Journaling

There is a huge amount of research around gratitude and how helpful it is for our mental well-being. For example, gratitude helps us build more positive relationships, reduces depression, increases resilience, improves physical health, reduces internal toxic emotions (i.e., increases empathy and decreases depression), and improves quality and quantity of sleep (to name just a few research findings).

How so? Gratitude journaling activates two different parts of the brain, the hypothalamus (the stress regulator) and the ventral tegmental area (the reward system activator). So at the same time that we are reducing stress, we are creating the sensation of winning a (little, tiny) lottery by increasing serotonin and dopamine (which is why some gratitude researchers call gratitude a "natural antidepressant").

None of this is to say that things can't be awful, or that work doesn't need to be done to make them un-awful. Gratitude doesn't replace social justice movements, advocacy, boundaries, and voice. Instead, it's about re-aligning ourselves with what is important. Gratitude is a remembrance of what we are fighting for, if we are in the midst of such a fight (and we kinda almost always are, right?).

So here's where gratitude journaling comes in. It's a structured way to incorporate gratitude into our daily lives. But how do you do it, exactly? I usually suggest writing in a gratitude journal as a daily practice, but also giving yourself a specific prompt to focus on each week (this helps you continue the practice long-term because it keeps your brain from getting bored with the routine). Here are some examples of prompts to try[11]:

- The small, daily comforts I am grateful for.

- The material items that make my life easier that I am grateful for.

- The beauty in the world that I am grateful for.

- The kindness of others that I am grateful for.

- The healthy stress-management skills I have that I am grateful for.

- The new skills I learned that I am grateful for.

- The tasks that I accomplished that I am grateful for.

- The future plans that I created that I am grateful for.

- The ways I've demonstrated compassion for others that I am grateful for.

- The self-care strategies that I utilized that I am grateful for.

- The positive cognitive shifts (thinking changes) that I am grateful for.

11 These are taken from my 2019 publication *12 Week Gratitude Journal*, which has some more helpful info on gratitude journaling. It's available on my website, faithgharper.com.

- The healthy boundaries that I have developed that I am grateful for.

Emotional Acupressure (EFT Tapping)

I am including this up top with the more inclusive techniques, because research also shows that it is helpful across the board, not just for some aspects of treatment as previously thought. I do not, however, have any evidence that the Navy SEALS use it themselves.

EFT is short for emotional freedom technique, a form of emotional acupressure or tapping. It is a self-care strategy that can work really well on a variety of issues. It is best known for treating anxiety and chronic pain and helping you awesome athletic types achieve peak performance. In a world of super-fancy (and super-expensive) therapies, this one is completely free and easy to learn, and it doesn't require props, equipment, or special workout clothes.

Emotional acupressure is a variation of energy psychology, which is based in theories that combine both Western and Eastern principles of the mind-body connection in order to facilitate healing. I had *never* heard anything about energy psychology until I was introduced to it in grad school close to a zillion years ago, although now books and documentaries and how-to YouTube videos are all over the place promoting different tapping interventions.

Tapping uses the same energy meridians used in traditional Chinese medicine (TCM) for the last 5,000 years. Unlike acupuncture, which uses needles, the work is done by tapping with your fingers. The tapping activates specific meridians on the head, chest, and hands by literally pushing down on them with your fingers.

While doing the tapping, you focus on a specific issue you are working to resolve. This could be chronic pain, a traumatic event, anxiety, depression, struggles with addictive behavior, etc. You will be acknowledging the event while focusing on your ability to restore balance in your body.

So if you are wondering, "You want me to TAP on my COLLARBONE while telling myself Stuart Smalley–type affirmations?" Kinda, yeah. When I first learned about it (again back when dinosaurs roamed the earth, and this modality was fairly new), I considered it another possible tool when a client and I were stuck, because at least it wouldn't cause any harm. So I tried it sometimes and people found it helpful. And over the years research began to build, including some sounder science on how and why the technique likely works. Currently, one of the emotional acupressure protocols, Thought Field Therapy (TFT), is listed on the National Registry of Evidence-Based Programs and Practices (NREPP) maintained by the Substance Abuse and Mental Health Services Administration. So it's more woo-woo than a traditional Western medicine practice, but it comes with the receipts.

To understand a little bit about how tapping might work, let's go back to the polyvagal theory stuff I've been yammering on about. A dense, nerdy polyvagal theory book edited by Stephen Porges (our polyvagal guru mentioned above) and Deb Dana (*Clinical Applications of the Polyvagal Theory*, if you're down) includes a chapter on emotional acupressure, noting that the gentle awakening of our electrical body is healing the flow of ventral vagal regulation. Meaning it is facilitating the body's ability to heal itself and regain stasis when outside events have disrupted our internal process.

Tapping helps keep the more evolved branches of the vagus nerve in charge of the situation, rather than having Uncle B come in with shotgun blasting all day, every day. It keeps the evolved branches activated, so your thinking brain is functioning. This is why EFT is so helpful for things like stress, anxiety, depression, PTSD, and other trauma responses.

Now, if you have ever had acupuncture done you know how complicated it is. There are 361 points (plus 36 extra points) that are used to impact blocked energy. But for the purpose of EFT, you just need to know about 12 meridians (six pairs) and two governing vessels that are interconnected. By stimulating certain points, we can send balancing energy down one pathway, influencing other pathways in the process.

Some of the research around energy medicine demonstrates how working with the energy meridians in the body is up to 10 times faster than even influencing the nervous system directly, which makes sense as we are starting to realize that the meridians are what we now refer to as a vascular system, and maybe 5,000-year-old traditional Chinese medicine has a lot going for it and this technique may feel silly but be of huge benefit.

How to Do EFT

So how do you actually use this as a coping skill? In this section, we're going to go over some basic focusing and tapping. There is a sequence involved that I'm going to walk you through below, with some basic illustrations showing where to tap and why it works.

If it all seems confusing, there are tons of videos on YouTube that show the process. Pull one up and check it out if you are having a hard time picturing how this all works. It can really help to see it in action!

1. Identify the Issue

What is the specific thing you want to work on? It could be a traumatic memory, chronic pain, or something that embarrassed you that you are still carrying. Just choose one single, easily defined issue to focus on—if you try to get complicated it won't work as well.

2. Rate the Intensity

Here you are just going to rate how strongly the issue is impacting you in the present on a scale of 0–10. Zero means no problem at all, and 10 is the worst it has ever felt.

This will help us figure out if the EFT is working for you, because the plan is to see the numbers decrease as you do the work.

If you are dealing with physical pain, rate the pain you are feeling at this time. If it's emotional, focus on the memories and rate how negative the memories make you feel.

3. Say the Setup

The setup is where you acknowledge the issue you are working on and accept yourself despite this issue that is currently getting in your way. While tapping the first point (the Karate Chop, or KC point), you will be saying a simple phrase to let your brain connect to your body over what you are intentionally working on.

The standard setup is the following:

"Even though I have this _____, I deeply and completely accept myself."

This is pretty basic. It's just a reminder to your system about what you are working on. It could be "this headache" or "this anxiety" or "this horrible memory." You are just creating a label for what you are struggling with.

I know, it's cheesy. You can totally play with the script if you want to . . . but the important part is to be earnest and sincere. Sarcasm font HAS to be off or you are just reinforcing the original issue by saying you don't quite trust the process. We're just trying new stuff here, right? Trust it enough to give it a real try.

I suggest trying the standard setup at first, and only adapting to fit your specific needs after you feel comfortable doing so. There is a huge power in how we talk to ourselves, so if your script isn't authentic, it really won't work.

It sounds weird, but you do want to focus on the negative. Even if you are using EFT to enhance performance, you are focusing on how you are not where you want to be yet. The idea is that this negativity is already there, blocking your energy, and we have to name it and claim it to clear it out of our bodies. Makes sense, right?

4. Do the Tapping Sequence

You are going to be using a portion of your setup script as you go through your tapping sequence, focusing on the negative you are trying to clear. Like I mentioned above, keep it super simple. Something like "this headache" works perfectly . . . unless of course a headache isn't your issue!

As you become more comfortable, or if you are working with a therapist who is trained in EFT, you may start playing with your setup script somewhat during your tapping sequence. I tend to adapt and prompt clients through scripts that really focus on their particular issue to help the process along.

The important thing is that you use your script (repeat what you are working on) throughout the tapping sequence, to help maintain your focus on what you are working on. Unlike with regular acupressure or acupuncture, you are adding direct mindfulness to the process so you remember what you are working on and why!

At the end of this chapter is a super fancy diagram I created with clip art and a Sharpie to help you visualize where all the tapping points are. I know, no expenses spared on high-tech graphics!

KC: The karate chop point is the starting point we use to let your body know we are about to do some work on your meridians! It is the part of your hand you would use if you were doing a karate chop . . . makes sense, right? The outside of your hand between your baby finger and your wrist has a soft, fleshy part . . . that's where you are going to tap (either hand is fine). Most people tap using their pointer and middle fingers, but figure out what feels most comfortable for you. You're tapping as you're repeating your script, as if you are tapping a friend on the shoulder for their attention. (And yes, the karate chop point is a TERRIBLE name. I use it only because it's the term that is used in all the EFT literature, and I was trying to be consistent. Which is a really dumb excuse. I'd love ideas for renaming this point, so send me any you have!)

TH: The literal middle of the top of your head. Easy, right?

EB: This is at the beginning of your eyebrow, right above it, just to the side of the nose. It's harder to find if you have a unibrow thing going on, so you can just go right above the edge of your eye socket (either eyebrow is fine).

SE: This means side of the eye. It's the outside corner of the eye (same eye as you used for your eyebrow). The edge of the eye socket bone. Those of you who can rock winged eyeliner may be familiar with it.

UE: This means under eye. On the bone at the bottom middle of your eye socket . . . about an inch below your actual pupil.

UN: This means under nose, that little dip between the bottom of your nose and the top of your lip. Word nerds? This area is called the philtrum. You are ready to be a contestant on *Jeopardy!* now.

CH: Midway between the point of your chin and the bottom of your lower lip. It's not technically on the chin, but chin makes it easy to remember. It's another little groove on the face, and it's actually called labiomental crease. You are going to totally wipe a whole category on *Jeopardy!* because of this!

CB: This stands for collarbone but actually is the area of the breastbone where the collarbone meets the first rib. So at the top of the breastbone is a U-shaped notch. Put your fingers there, then go down an inch and over an inch (to either the left or the right). Once you hit the right spot, it will be easy to find again. The area we are aiming for is a bundle of nerves called the brachial plexus. Daily Double time!

UA: This stands for under the arm. It's the side of the body, about four inches below the armpit. If you wear a bra, it will be about the middle of your bra band. If you are flat chested it will be the point that's even with where your nipple is or would be.

5. Notice the Aspects

Stuff comes up when you do this—stuff that you didn't realize was there—and sometimes doing EFT can be triggering at first. In EFT these hidden components of a problem are called aspects.

A lot of times we may hit upon one of these aspects without realizing it in a session. You may hit on one of these aspects and the intensity of what you are feeling actually increases.

That's OK, though. If something comes up, you can focus on that aspect as its own singular issue, giving it its own setup and working through each aspect as a unique and individual issue.

6. Reevaluate the Issues and Aspect

Now you are going to evaluate your original issue on a 0–10 scale in terms of intensity.

If new aspects come up, assess their intensity separately and work on them as individual issues. As long as you keep noting some kind of intensity, you know that there is still something to work on. Once you think all the aspects have resolved, check the intensity of the initial issue and see if anything is left to work on.

Just like with the aspects, any intensity sensations left mean that the initial issue is still something you are working on. And that's OK . . . you may get it to a manageable point, and that's completely legit. You may have it flare up sometime in the future and want to use EFT to bring it back down to a manageable level.

If you find that the issue doesn't resolve completely or permanently, it may be helpful to keep a record of the circumstances in which it flares up and the intensity you note for it.

When all aspects seem to be resolved, you assess a new 0–10 number for the overall issue and see if there is anything left.

Putting It All Together

1. Identify the issue.

2. Rate the intensity.

3. Go through the setup using your script.

4. Go through the tapping sequence, continuing to use your script.

5. Rerate the intensity. Check for aspects that need to be worked through with a new setup, altering your script as needed.

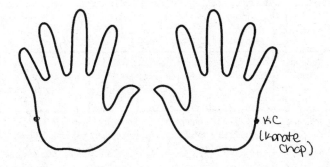

So How Do These Points Relate to Traditional Chinese Medicine?

EFT Point	Related TCM Point	Releases	Allows
TH (Top of Head)	Governing Vessel	Inner critic, lack of focus, and "hamster on a wheel" thinking	Insight, intuition, spiritual connection, focus, wisdom, spiritual discernment, and clarity
EB (Eyebrow)	Bladder Meridian	Trauma, hurt, sadness, restlessness, impatience, frustration, and dread	Inner peace and emotional healing
SE (Side of Eye)	Gall Bladder Meridian	Rage, anger, resentment, fear of change, and muddled thinking	Clarity, compassion, and understanding
UE (Under Eye)	Stomach Meridian	Fear, anxiety, worry, emptiness, nervousness, and disappointment	Contentment, calming, sense of safety
UN (Under Nose)	Governing Meridian	Embarrassment, shame, guilt, grief, fear of ridicule, powerlessness, fear of failure, and psychological reversals	Self-empowerment, self-acceptance, compassion for self and others
CH (Chin)	Conception Vessel	Confusion, uncertainty, embarrassment, shame, and second-guessing decisions	Certainty, clarity, self-confidence, and self-acceptance
CB (Collarbone)	Kidney Meridian (Adrenals)	Psychological reversal, worry, indecision, feeling stuck, and general stress	Ease in moving forward, confidence, and clarity
UA (Under Arm)	Spleen Meridian	Guilt, obessing, worry, hopelessness, insecurity, and poor self-esteem	Clarity, confidence, relaxation, and compassion for self and others

You will notice that the (horribly named) karate chop point is not on this list because it is the one point that does not correspond to an energy meridian in the human body.

Also, special thanks to George Tabares, DACM, L.Ac., for his assistance with this chart. He helped me even though I told him I would publicly blame him for anything that ends up being wrong on it. So he's both deeply patient and a brilliant traditional Chinese medicine practitioner. You can learn more about his services at tabaresactivehealth.com.

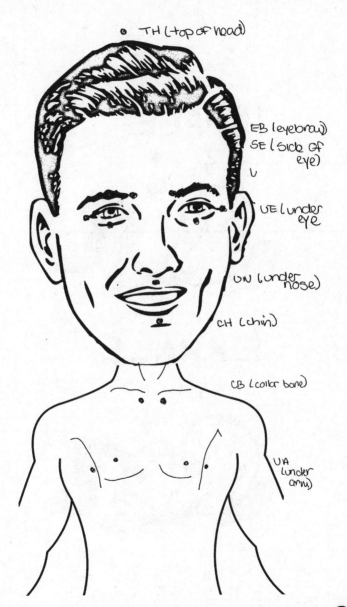

TH (top of head)

EB (eyebrow)
SE (side of eye)

UE (under eye)

UN (under nose)

CH (chin)

CB (collar bone)

UA (under arm)

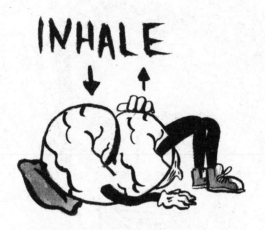

CHAPTER 5:
COPING SKILLS FOR *RIGHT NOW*

*I*n *Stress Coping Skills Deck* (the card deck I created as a companion tool for this book), the cards were split into two categories, surviving and thriving, for the sake of simplicity. This chapter is very much in line with the "surviving" cards from the deck. Getting through daily existence is always our first priority. *Then* we can get skillful about more transformational strategies to really thrive. There is a metaphor that is often used in therapy, especially in disordered eating recovery work, that applies to this concept.

Think of your stress levels as a rushing river. Especially if you are dealing with burnout, traumatic stress, or survival mode. You're trying to get to the other side, but instead you fall in. You're trying to get across the current, but instead it's carrying you downstream and you're in danger of drowning and getting increasingly exhausted. A log floats by and you grab onto it. You're able to haul yourself up a little bit and let the log keep you propped up. You are no longer in danger of drowning, and you get a little bit of rest and recovery since you aren't having to push across the current.

Problem is you're still in the river and you are still getting carried downstream instead of across to where you really want to go. Once you have caught your breath a little, you will be able to let go of the log and push off to the other bank again (and that is the part that comes next). But no matter what happens, anytime you hit another river with a hard current, you will know how to use a log to give yourself a little support in the moment.

Live Through This Skills

This is the catchall for all the ways we just manage our own activation and responses to whatever stress, grossness, and fuckery has been dished out to us without completely losing our minds. These are what therapists usually call "distress tolerance" skills.

These skills are about managing shitty feeling-thoughts. Not trying to unpack them or challenge them or change them in any way. Just to go, "Oh yeah, this feels like shit. But I can deal with this. Feeling-thoughts are just information from my body that bad shit is going down. They won't last forever. I can pay attention to them without falling apart."

Grounding Techniques

Grounding techniques are one of those things I yammer on about all the damn time. Because they WORK and they're SIMPLE and they help us remain in the present moment in our bodies and be aware of our surroundings. If you are a trauma survivor (and hey there, aren't we all??) then it's really easy to start reliving a past experience when shit is getting tough in the present. Grounding techniques are one of those can-do-anywhere coping skills that cost nothing and don't make you look obviously odd if you are using them while sitting on the bus.

Mental Grounding

Mental grounding techniques are intended to keep you in the present moment by focusing your attention on your current situation and surroundings. That includes anything that helps you remind yourself of where you are in the moment and that you have some control over your feeling-thoughts even though your stress reaction has been tripped.

- Use a phrase or mantra that is soothing to you. Navy SEAL positive-self-talk style. It could be "I got this" or "This is temporary" or "This may pass like a fucking kidney stone, but it WILL pass." Whatever works for you.

- Play a categories game with yourself. Name all your favorite shows, movies, books, songs, etc. The point is to draw from semantic memory instead of emotional memory.

- Describe something in great detail that is attached to the present moment. It may be all the colors you can see in front of you or an article you are holding in your hand.

- Go over your schedule in your mind, or the steps it takes to complete an activity you do well. This is accessing procedural memory, which is a declarative form of memory just like semantic memory . . . which helps you detach from the emotional memory being triggered.

Physical Grounding

It's the most amazing magic trick ever when we first realize as children that we can check out mentally from where we are physically. Teacher droning on and on? Totally just mentally escape to the playground. Then as we get older we realize "Oh,

SHIT! Now I'm doing this automatically! Even when I don't wanna! How do I get back in my body?" Physical grounding techniques do just that thing.

- Notice your breath. Just the physical in-and-out breathing experience. When your mind starts to wander, go back to the breath.

- Walk mindfully. Notice every step you take and the feeling when your foot connects to the earth. If your mind starts wandering away from you, you can always try holding a teaspoon of water while walking and focus on not spilling the water.

- Touch objects around you.

- Jump up and down.

- Eat something mindfully, attending to the flavors and textures.

- Make sure your feet are touching the floor. Try taking off your shoes and feeling the ground beneath you.

- If someone else touching you feels safe, have them put their hands on your shoulders and remind you to ground back in your body.

Square Breathing

Who else learned to breathe by sucking in their stomachs and filling their lungs deeply? Didn't we all? Isn't it a great irony (in the Alanis Morissette sense of the word) that this is exactly the opposite of how you should use breathing to calm yourself down? In order to get the most calming effect and encourage our brain waves to operate in alpha state (relaxed and focused), we should breathe from our bellies. If you've never done that before, lie down and put a stuffed animal or something else lightweight on your stomach and breathe deeply enough to see it move. That's the kind of breathing that is a functional coping skill.

Square breathing comes from dialectical behavior therapy and is a fairly simple expansion of the Navy SEAL breathing technique mentioned above:

- Breathe in for a count of four.

- Hold it for a count of four.

- Breathe out for a count of four.

- And hold one more time for a count of four.

Then repeat the sequence three more times (and yes, you did the math right . . . for a total of FOUR). You can totally do it longer than that if it's helping you. But give it at least a full cycle of four before checking in on your stress level.

Pendulation and Titration

Something acts as a stressor or a traumatic event reminder. You start noticing thoughts, feelings, sensations, and physical responses associated with elevated uncomfortable emotions and unhelpful behavioral impulses. These aren't positive sensations, so you go from just fine to totally dysregulated in under a minute, right?

Sensations language helps us recognize what's going on in our body, even when words fail. (And there's a reason words fail: the region of the brain responsible for language, known as Broca's area, goes inactive in a trauma response.) Once we start to connect to the sensations we feel when our trauma response is triggered, we can better control our response.

Pendulation work was developed by Peter Levine (mentioned earlier in this book—the writer of *Waking the Tiger,* among other books), whose work is focused on the somatic experience of trauma. That is, *how we hold trauma in our body*.

Pendulation starts with connecting to the sensations you feel in your body, especially when you are activated. But rather than staying in that place, you identify a space of calmness and safety. It's often referred to as an oasis (think of where you draw water from in the desert, when you are dying of thirst), a pool of resources, or your natural supports.

Pendulation is the action of teaching yourself to move out of the activated sensations and into your space of calmness. The idea is that we all have a safe space inside ourselves that we can draw strength from if we remember it's there. And it can help you gain mastery over the activation and learn to tolerate the sensations and feelings associated with activation for longer periods of time. And titration operates within that framework as a way of managing the flow. All titration means is slowing down the process. Stress is too much, too fast, all at once, and titration is a way of managing all our feels, one baby step at a time. It is our conscious effort to slow everything down so we can deal with it in manageable chunks. Titration is the pause we take to learn our bodies' responses better.

So when you start recognizing that you are activated, you can let yourself feel the negatives, and then remind yourself that you can intentionally move to your space of calmness and gather resources to process and release your experiences piece by piece.

Once you start to find ways to tolerate your activation, it no longer owns you. It no longer hijacks the entirety of your being, which means you are able to start managing your responses and operate from your prefrontal cortex again, and the activation starts to dissipate.

Pendulation Exercise
It sounds weird until you try it a couple of times, so here is a step-by-step guide. And if you don't want to write in a perfectly lovely book, you can download my worksheet version of this exercise from my website (faithgharper.com).

Start by scanning your body to figure out which areas feel safe and secure for you and which tend to get activated when you are stressed. I tend to feel stress in my stomach, while others feel it in their neck and shoulders, for example. Try using the following color codes to mark where you feel the most activated (anxious, angry, upset) in your body, and where you feel the most calm. This information will help you deliberately connect to, and feel calmer during, times when you are highly activated by intentionally stepping into your calm space until the highest-level sensations are able to discharge and dissipate.

Red – The places that feel high-range activated

Orange – The places that feel medium-range activated

Yellow – The places that feel low-range activated

Green – The places that feel neutral

Blue – The places that feel calm

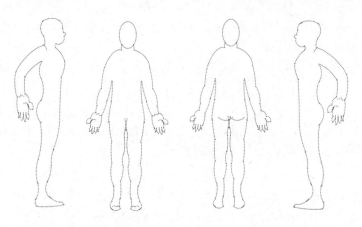

You may not be really sure where your places are, especially if you have disassociated from your body sensations in order to get through life without a total breakdown. That's entirely OK, and makes perfect sense . . . but here is your chance to start trying to connect to those sensations throughout the days and weeks ahead. If you have a therapist you are working with, you can incorporate this work into therapy.

Once you have a good idea of where you feel most safe in your body and where you feel most activated, the pendulation exercise is designed to help you move back and forth so you can experience feeling intense emotions without having them completely take over.

You start with the part of your body that feels safe (the oasis space). For me, that's always my chest . . . in my heart and in my breath. Then you move your awareness into the activated space. For me, that would be my stomach, like I mentioned. Approach the activated space gently, with neutrality and curiosity about the experience, rather than anxiety, anger, embarrassment, and shame. For example:

"Hey there stomach, you're upset with me today. I can tell. I'm aware. Thank you for letting me know. I want you to feel safe, but you don't get to take over and be in charge."

Then you move back to the safe space . . . in your body. For me (again), it's a return to my breath.

It sounds woo-woo, but really all you're doing is teaching your brain to manage the sensations in your body. To invite them into consciousness without letting them go into hostile takeover mode. And learning to experience them without a constant sense of being overwhelmed.

The rhythm of moving back and forth through internal states will influence the vagus nerve and the connective tissue throughout your body, which will help flush out the stress hormones and help turn off the physiological trigger response that was activated in you.

Here's a little step-by-step summary:

1. When you find yourself activated, notice where it is in your body. Do you feel tense? Shaky? Completely numb?

2. Where in your body do you feel safest or at least neutral?

3. Practice focusing on the activated feelings, then moving slowly to focus on the safer feelings. As you practice and feel in control of the movement, you can spend more time on the activated feelings, showing yourself that they are manageable and will dissipate.

Open Hand/Closed Hand
This is a far simpler body awareness exercise that works really well if the pendulation and titration exercise is either too much

to handle or too complicated to figure out. And because you are focusing on your hands, you are less likely to activate your sympathetic nervous system through the vagus nerve, and therefore less likely to accidentally become triggered.

1. Hold out one of your hands. It doesn't matter which one, but pay attention to your natural inclination.

2. Hold it in the air, without letting it rest against another surface (like your leg or the table in front of you), if you are able to do so without pain.

3. Open your hand up, facing back towards you so you have the palm of your hand directly in your line of sight.

4. While watching your hand, slowly make it into a fist. Notice the difference in the sensation between what it felt like open and what it feels like closed.

5. Maintaining eye contact, open your hand back up.

6. Now close your eyes and repeat this sequence. Notice what it feels like from the inside (the closing and opening of your hand).

What felt different? How did your awareness of the experience change once you were entirely dependent on your internal sense messages? Was it disconcerting at any point? Comforting? Did anything shift in how you connect with your body?

Even More Here-And-Now, Short-Term, Instant-Gratification Coping Skills

The more coping skills you have in your back pocket, the better. If you have an array of stuff to draw from, you are far less likely to fall apart. Consider it a toolbox. You may have a really fantastic screwdriver. Passed down for generations. Your grandpa used it to fix the bathtub 60 years ago. That's all well and good, except maybe it's a flat head and today is the day you need a Phillips head. My suggestion? Try any of the following skills that sound vaguely interesting, useful, or intriguing. There is nothing wrong with having a huge, rolling cart of tools on hand at all times. And these are the types of skills that you can use in the moment when you are about to lose your shit. They don't require as much planning, practice, and implementation as many of the others discussed above.[12]

1. Chew on something. Gum. Beef jerky. Pop Rocks. Something that you can focus your attention on.

2. Find something to keep your hands busy. Stuff like Play-Doh or Silly Putty is less distracting than fidget spinners, Slinkys, fidget cubes, etc. But dude, use whatever works for ya.

3. Blink. It interrupts the brain's perception of time (according to research, it may function as a way of slowing down our neural metabolism). It's essentially a system reboot/mini-nap that we do throughout our waking hours unconsciously and that we can also do consciously when stressed.

4. Attach a specific scent to feeling calm, happy, and relaxed (lavender can be a good one to use since it has calming properties in its own right). You do this by intentionally smelling a certain scent when you feel safe and relaxed. Like after meditation or guided imagery or exercising. Then carry a drop of that scent on a cotton ball in a ziplock baggie or small container. When feeling

12 This list of quick-and-dirty coping skills is also available online at Microcosm. Pub/QuickCopingSkills.

stressed, open it and inhale the scent and reconnect to the calm feeling.

5.   When you find yourself thinking in negative terms of "I can'ts" (such as "I can't deal with large crowds" or "I can't run a 10K") add the word " . . . yet" to the end of the thought. That opens you up to the possibility of working towards being able to do it later, rather than getting stuck in a cycle of negativity.

6.   Take a hot bath with Epsom salts for a detox. If you don't have access to a tub, at least soak your feet.

7.   Go ahead and cry. Sad tears release chemicals that other tears do not.

8.   Create a list, either in your head or written down, of five things you are grateful for. (My mom made me do this when I was little and I hated her for it . . . but it so worked.)

9.   Take off your shoes and socks and connect to the ground beneath you. (It's called "earthing"—the idea is connecting to the earth more than your own body, which is grounding.)

10. Hold a piece of ice in your hand. It won't actually hurt you, but the sensation will disrupt the other distress signals in your body. This is an especially good coping skill if you struggle with thoughts of self-injury.

11. Count backwards from 100 by threes. Trust me, you won't be able to focus on anything but keeping those numbers organized in your mind.

12. Look at cat videos online. Or pygmy goat videos. Or panda bears. Or puppy dogs. Embrace whatever your cuteness kryptonite is for a defined break (like five minutes, as you will see in the Pomodoro Technique later in this book).

13. Identify whatever muscles are tense in your body and intentionally relax them one by one.

14. Visualize a stop sign in your head. And tell yourself "STOP."

15. Picture an ideal moment in your life. Put yourself back in that experience and connect to the positive feelings you associate with that time period.

16. Blow bubbles. It's damn impossible to have panic-attack-inducing breathing and control your breath enough to blow a bubble at the same time.

17. Get under something heavy. Weighted blankets are great, but whatever blankets you have will also do, so pile them on you. Or crawl between the mattress and the box spring of your bed, if that won't induce any claustrophobic feelings. As a general rule, you want a weighted blanket to be 10% of your body weight if you are an adult for maximum effect. For kiddos, it's about 10% of their current body weight plus a pound or two.

18. Sit in the sun. Vitamin D helps depression symptoms and reduces systemic inflammation in the body.

19. Do some gentle yoga poses (also known as forms, or by their Sanskrit word, asanas). These facilitate body awareness. (If the pendulation / titration exercises seem

really difficult, the asanas can help move you in that direction.)

20. Drink something warm and soothing. Coffee or tea with honey and lemon. Do caffeine-free if caffeine makes you edgy (my personal favorite comfort tea is Good Earth Sweet & Spicy, and it is available with caffeine and without).

21. Take a picture of a living thing that you love. Your boo. Your kiddo (human or fur baby). Your bestie. A gorgeous flower. Your own damn rock-star survivor self. Take pictures of all of them. Remind yourself that there is love and beauty living out in the world.

22. Create a tiny treats budget and hit the thrift or dollar store. When I was raising my daughter on 18k a year and living off my WIC groceries, one of my favorite treat activities was to buy a dollar bottle of nail polish and give myself a pedi at home. Create a tiny fun budget for yourself. Something in the one-to-five-dollar range maybe? Hit the dollar store or resale shop and treat yourself to something that's purely for fun. A bubble bath. A cheesy book. A new mug for your Sweet & Spicy tea.

23. Write a letter to someone you love or appreciate. Tell them what makes them so special to you. You can send it or not, but sending it might turn out to be the boost THEY need.

24. Write a letter to yourself. Your past self, your future self, your current self. Who could use some support and words of wisdom?

25.   Take one toxic (or suspicious) thing out of your life for 21 days. A food, a substance, a shitty human being. How do you feel? Any better? What happens when you allow it (or them) back in three weeks later? Does your body say no?

26.   Drink some water. Drink A LOT of water. I don't wanna see one bit of yellow in that pee, OK? Water is as vital to the brain as it is to the body. It improves our memory and our concentration. You NEED those brain cells well lubricated, am I right?

27.   Reflect on something you do hella well. How'd you get so good at it? How might those skills translate to this situation?

28.   Make a list of things that DON'T need to be changed in your life. What works just fucking fine?

29.   Have sex, cuddle with someone, get a light touch massage, or just *think* about someone you feel close to. These are all activities that release oxytocin (deep tissue massage decreases cortisol, but light touch massage releases far more oxytocin). Oxytocin is a peptide hormone that facilitates connection and empathy. Interesting thing? While cis women are the people scientists have said have more access to (and therefore more) oxytocin (thanks to childbirth, nursing, and a higher likelihood of being relational in general), cis men are far more sensitive to oxytocin than cis women. We all need it to keep our parasympathetic nervous system online!

30. Touch not an option? Nurture relationships in other ways. Send someone a text or email thanking them or telling them how much you appreciate them. Deepening our connection with people has a stronger positive correlation to our health than smoking has to cancer!

31. Strike a (power) pose. Tons of research shows that when we stand like superheroes (legs apart, hands on hips) we feel more powerful. Standing like this for two minutes decreases cortisol (the stress hormone) and increases testosterone (our engaged-to-win hormone). Channel your inner Wonder Woman or Black Panther, y'all.

32. Take a tech break (and can I just say I initially typed this as "brake," which is equally appropriate). Set up a schedule for checking your messages and social media rather than being on the obsessive constant tech check. Some people have gone so far as to gray out their phone screens (without the bright colors to entice us, we are far less likely to fall back into the rabbit hole of mindless scrolling).

33. Picture someone or something that represents loving-kindness and compassion to you. It could be a person, a spiritual figure, or maybe an aspect of nature that resonates with you. Picture yourself in the presence of this compassion and loving-kindness and feel these things towards yourself. What would you hear? How would these experiences feel to you?

34. Try a Tibetan singing bowl. The concentration it takes to make it hum is sort of like blowing bubbles. You

have to focus so much on that, you can't focus on other stuff. (I have a friend with a neurological tremor who can focus in well enough to hold his fingers still with the bowl, and that's AMAZING. It's the only time I've seen him not shake!)

35. Do something slowly. Like, slow way down and be mindful. Or pick a task that requires time and mindful attention (making risotto works, trust me on this one!).

36. Plan a dream trip. Is it a vacation or a learning experience? Where will you go? What will you do? Most importantly, what amazing foods will you try? Plan out all the details . . . you've now got an amazing goal to work toward!

37. Pick an anthem song. Play that shit when you need a pick-me-up. Sing along LOUD. (Mine is "Sunflowers" by the Velvet Janes.)

38. Smudge that shit. Seriously, the research shows that burning sage and other herbs kills toxins in the air and improves brain functions. Obvs, burning and producing smoke is better (and that's what I do at home), but at work I use a sage spray so I don't set off the smoke detectors in the building (everyone there already has enough to put up with having me around!).

39. Set your intention by saying it out loud, not just thinking it. It adds an auditory cue, making it more likely to stick.

40. Do 5-7-8 breathing. You are essentially breathing in for five counts, holding for seven, exhaling for eight. The longer exhale engages the parasympathetic response.

41. Take a break from your comfort zone. Take a different route, even if just to your mailbox. Chew your food on the other side of your mouth (you have no IDEA how weird that will feel to do intentionally if you are a creature of habit!). Pay attention to how these changes affect you; it gives you something new to focus on.

42. Make a list of things you look forward to. If the list seems small, create new things to look forward to, like a cupcake date with yourself at the end of the week. Anticipation produces dopamine before you even get the reward!

43. Are you really furious about something? Try the 60-minute "anger package" from Julia Samuel's book *Grief Works*. Do 10 minutes of journaling, 20 minutes of running (or some other cardio exercise), 10 minutes of meditating, and 20 minutes of watching or reading something funny.

44. Shift your language. Say "I don't" instead of "I can't." Instead of making demands of others, state your preference to them and label it as such. These language shifts add ownership to your experience and decrease the power struggle.

45. Make one small but healthy change for 21 days and see how you feel after. Not a huge diet shift, but maybe switch out dairy milk for almond milk. Maybe do five minutes of stretching in the morning before going to work. Maybe switch to half-caff instead of fully caffeinated coffee. Something that can have a huge impact without a ton of extra stress and planning.

46. Try a cue-controlled relaxation technique. Just tense and then relax certain muscles in your body at a time, so you can connect and feel the difference. When we are upset, we tense our muscles in certain patterns as part of our fight-flight-freeze response. By connecting back to our bodies, we can start to unpack these patterns so when they occur we know where to focus our relaxation efforts.

47. Channel your inner Dr. Phil. Step outside what's going on mentally for a moment and ask yourself, booming Texas drawl included, "How's that workin' for ya?" This isn't intended as a mechanism of self-shaming for whatever response you are having. Remember, responses aren't good or bad, they are all adaptive. But this does let you step out of the cycle of response for a minute and judge whether it's an adaptation that is helping you through the current situation in the healthiest way possible. So you can adjust as need be.

CHAPTER 6:
INTERNAL JUDO:
SHIFTING YOUR
THOUGHTS

Remember all my annoying metaphors from the previous chapter? About moving from surviving to thriving? And grabbing onto a log? The last chapter was all about staying afloat in the moment, and now we're going to focus more on getting to the other side of the river. That's the point of the skills in this chapter: not just surviving in the here-and-now, but figuring out how to work *with* our own reactions to mitigate distress.

I stole the term "internal judo" from Aaron Sapp, my ever-patient friend and collaborator. The skills in this category are about evaluating our internal responses (thoughts or feelings). While everything we feel is real, it may not always reflect the complexity of reality. And even if your internal thought process represents the truthiest truth in the history of all that is accurate about the universe, that doesn't mean that you are entirely stuck with the exact story you've got going on right now. Feeling-thoughts may be accurate, but not the least bit fucking helpful.

These skills are the ones where you recognize your feeling-thoughts and work to unpack them a bit. Or reframe them just enough to create some breathing room. Sometimes coping means recognizing the fuckery going on but distancing ourselves from it mentally.

Mindset

Research supports that we have far more control over our experience of stress and how it affects our bodies than you'd think. This control comes not from chucking everything and living in a van down by the river, but from changing your *perception* of stress.

Remember how we talked earlier about how stress is just your body perceiving that something is important and upping its resource game? Some smart people compared data from the National Health Interview Survey to data on mortality in the US. Guess what they found? Stress alone isn't so bad for you. But if you think that stress is bad for your health *and* you perceive yourself as having a lot of stress, you have way worse physical and mental health outcomes. These individuals had a 43% higher risk of premature death than folks who didn't have these perceptions. This seems mean spirited and victim-blamey toward our own bodies. But evolutionarily speaking, it's a feature, not a bug. Our mindset helps our chances of survival, so our body rewards us for having a positive one.

So if you *think* about stress in a negative way you are far more likely to die of a stress-related disease.

There are tons of studies of this nature, if you start digging. In 1998, 30,000 adults in the US were asked about the levels of stress in their life and whether or not they felt that stress was harmful to their health. Eight years later, researchers scoured public records to see which of the 30,000 had died. High levels of stress increased the risk of dying by 41%, but only if these same people believed that stress was harmful to their health. Stress *plus* the belief that stress is harmful is what makes stress the 15th leading cause of death in the US. Our belief system has more impact on our longevity than quitting smoking or taking up exercise: while exercising and smoking cessation are consistently shown to add four years to our lives, having a positive outlook on aging adds eight, according to a Yale study cited in *The Upside of Stress* by Kelly McGonigal.

And several of the studies show that there is a cascading effect on our behaviors, not just our health. For example, one study of Crohn's patients found that a patient's perception of their illness had a direct effect on their stress levels *and* their stress levels had a direct impact on the types of coping skills they used. That is, the more stressed they were, the more likely they were to use coping skills that were more harmful and costly in the long run, such as disordered eating, dissociating via overuse of social media and the internet, and abuse of drugs and alcohol.

Consider your own history with stress:

- What kinds of avoidant coping skills have you used in the past?

- What other kinds of coping skills have you used that aren't avoidant of the stressor but are ultimately unhealthy for you?

- What opportunities have you missed in an attempt to avoid the stress that would come along with them?

- How might you be limiting your future?

Embracing challenges and facing the problems in our lives proactively increases our likelihood of remaining in our ventral vagal zone of tolerance. We know that the opposite of fight/flight is rest/digest in its passive state, but it is also known as tend/befriend in its active state. Meaning we are engaged in connection with others toward the betterment of all. The people who have suffered the most in life are also the people who jump in to care for others. Stress can actually increase our courage and our capacity for caregiving and strengthen our social relationships. Changing our individual lives, as well as the world around us, requires us to have a mindful relationship with our stress response.

Embracing Stress Through Mindset Training

The author of *The Upside of Stress*, Kelly McGonigal (whose research is the starting point for a lot of what I write about here), states: *"Embracing stress is a radical act of self-trust."*

We've been told not to though, haven't we? We're told to avoid stress, to calm down, that it isn't good for us. Dr. McGonigal also cites Harvard Business School professor Alison Wood Brooks, who asked hundreds of people the same question: If you are anxious about a big presentation, what's a better way of handling it? Feeling excited or trying to calm down?

91% of people said "trying to calm down."

But, as mentioned eleventy times above, the stress isn't harmful in and of itself—it's not necessarily a problem you need to solve or get away from. This is borne out by multiple studies, including the one mentioned above, where the researchers found that just saying "I'm excited" out loud can reappraise stress as excitement. Despite what most of us have been told, it's easier for the brain to jump from anxious feelings to excited ones rather than to calm ones. Cortisol is going to be activated because something matters to you. But you can consciously label the feeling as excited instead of stressed, which changes how you interpret and experience your own body.

The practice of reframing our thoughts from those of overwhelm to those of empowerment is known as mindset training. This doesn't mean bullshitting ourselves, but recognizing that we do have the capacity to handle tough situations, or at least the capacity to give it our all and try our best. The term mindset is one of those words we associate with those performance-coach guru types. Tony Robbins isn't wrong, though. Mindsets are really nothing more than the beliefs we have about ourselves and the world that shape our realities. This isn't negating the fact that we may be dealing with really fucked-up situations, but it is about taking back whatever power we have in our own responses when dealing with shitshow scenerios.

Mindset training has a direct impact on our stress response. One study found that a stronger physical stress response was associated with higher test scores in school situations, but only for people who have had mindset training. Another study demonstrated that just telling people "You're the kind of person whose performance improves under pressure" increases their task performance by 33%. One of the biggest predictors of stress overwhelming us is our perception of not being up to the task, so our thinking shifts when we focus on the fact that we are, indeed, up to it.

And yes, individuals with anxiety can absolutely benefit from mindset training. Since stress is one of the biggest anxiety triggers, researchers have demonstrated that the stress response (at least the beginning of it) is the same for people who have anxiety and those who do not. It's our perception of what it means that differs. So a disruption of that stress response can end up circumventing anxiety and panic attacks.

Psychology researcher Salvatore Maddi termed this mindset-building a form of hardiness, meaning the courage to grow from stress. This is how someone can be "good at stress." It doesn't mean that difficulties don't get to us and stress doesn't bother us, but rather that we value growth, accomplishment, and being an active participant in our own lives enough that we befriend our stress response when we can and learn from it when it overwhelms us.

Any stressful situation can become an opportunity to practice a mindset shift. When you notice your stress response activating, you can remind yourself that your body is reacting to something *because it's important to you*. Then, use that energy to help carry you through the situation. Whether you are getting through a stressful interview or fighting fascism, being alert, engaged, and present is vital to success.

Mindset training seems awkward at first, but once you build that neural pathway it becomes more natural and more likely to be your automatic response. As you practice, you won't have to work so hard at it over time. Your stress mindset will also change how you react to others' stress. Mindset is connected with resilience. And because emotional resilience is one of the first lines of defense against mental illnesses like depression, learning what behaviors build emotional resilience could clue physicians in to how to treat those illnesses.

Having a GOOD Mindset

You can practice mindset training as part of your daily self-care routine. I like the GOOD acronym for mindset training since it doesn't involve any kind of fake hype about shitty situations; it really is just about being grounded in your own self-efficacy. And clearly you are a fucking survivor—you're reading this right now, which means your survival rate thus far is 100%, right? This is one of those internal work exercises that might be easier to make external by journaling through it, especially at first while you get used to the process. But I am, for once, not insisting you write everything down if you really hate that shit!

- **Gratitude:** As we learned in the section on gratitude journaling in Chapter 4, focusing on gratitude is a really important part of our mental health in general and can create a perspective shift in our day. This doesn't mean discounting what's problematic, but rather focusing more on what's good in your life.

- **Openness to Possibilities:** If we are gratitude focused, we are far more likely to be aware of solutions, support, and opportunities around us. In a negative mindset, we are more likely to dismiss things that are available to us (or not notice them at all) because we are overwhelmed and frustrated with life in general.

- **Opportunities in This Experience:** No matter what experience we are having, we can focus on the opportunities that exist to help us grow. We can learn more about different situations and ourselves even if we don't achieve the success we were hoping for. As someone who does a lot of political advocacy work, I can tell you that every lost battle taught me a new strategy of approach for next time.

- **Determine:** Visualize yourself successfully embracing the challenges ahead. This is hardiness in action. If you mentally set yourself up for success, you are in the right frame of mind to tackle the project. And no, you aren't more frustrated if things don't go perfectly. I've found that even when I don't succeed, I'm still proud of myself for going in prepared and positive because I feel like I really gave it my all.

Curiosity and Neutrality

We tend to label things as good or bad, wanted or unwanted. Approaching life with curiosity and neutrality shuts up our internal judge and jury. *Curiosity* means just applying the question "Oh, interesting, I wonder where that is coming from?" to both the behaviors of others and our own thoughts and feelings. It allows us to pay attention and look for clues that explain what's going on.

Often clients will come in and tell me a story, ending it with " . . . and they TOTALLY did XXX for YYY reason!" My response is usually to the tune of "Oh, wow. Well you know them better than I do, but when you were telling me the story I couldn't help but wonder if they were doing XXX for another reason, such as . . ." It's tough, when you are actively mad at someone, not to ascribe malicious intent to their behavior. But truly, not everyone is going around plotting and scheming like a cartoon villain. It doesn't change the outcome of the behavior, but it may make coping with the behavior far easier . . . and help facilitate a conversation so that it doesn't happen again.

Neutrality is a mental-shifting exercise that really helps with all behaviors and intentions, but especially your own. When you can't find the good in a situation, and you have no energy for active curiosity, you can actively label it as neutral and move on. It's not good or bad, *it just is what it is*. It exists and you are going to contend with it. You don't have to take ownership of it as being directed toward making your life difficult or some repayment of your karmic debt. And if it is inward negative messaging that you can't switch off? Start by trying to have a more neutral interaction with yourself. Positive may be difficult if you have years of negative programming. Neutral will give you a measure of relief and may be far more doable in the present.

The Art of Doing Nothing: An Intervention

Metacognitive therapy (MCT) was designed by Adrian Wells based on information processing theory, with the idea that we are bigger than the sum of our parts and that our mind is able to observe what the brain is doing at any given moment. This makes sense, right? Even when our brains are tripping balls, we have an awareness that it is happening. Dr. Wells thought, "What if we focus on what the mind is noticing and use the mind to guide the brain away from the fixated thought loops that cause us worry and rumination?"

Self-regulation is what we do when we shift the focus of our thoughts and feelings and behaviors in more helpful directions. In my clinical practice, I call it "self-coaching," referring to our inner dialogue about our focus and goals related to big things and little everyday things. Science-y explanation? Keeping our prefrontal cortex online allows us to self-regulate by developing a sense of mastery over the subcortical regions of the brain involved in reward (the striatum, etc.) and emotion (our asshole friend the amygdala, etc.).

Metacognitive therapy was initially designed to be used with depression and anxiety. But research shows it also to be helpful for more generalized stress, as in a study where MCT techniques were taught to individuals with workplace stressors.

Backstory on all that is important, not just cuz we're big ole nerds together, but also to explain that when I suggest practicing doing "nothing," I'm not being sarcastic, flippant, or self-gaslight-y. Because one of the things that is incredibly beneficial in MCT is something that is referred to as detached mindfulness. The idea is that we all have negative thoughts and feelings, and getting stuck in the cycles of them either creates mental discomfort or continues to fuel whatever mental discomfort our janky brain chemicals have already created.

We aren't trying to escape negative thoughts, we're just trying not to connect to them as true, real, or worthy of our attention. My fellow Buddhists may recognize this as working with shenpa. As Pema Chödrön has noted, shenpa is often translated as "attachment," but the better word would be "hooked." We get hooked into the asshole things our brains say, which feeds our more unhelpful habit loops. When these thoughts arise the idea is to do the following:

- Take a step back from them. It may help to create a strategy to remind yourself to do this. In hypnotherapy, one technique we use is to think of our thoughts as something that exists on a movie screen, while we sit in the audience watching the images move across the screen. So you're not trying to control them (which is like saying "don't think of an elephant!" because of course you just did), you're just viewing them as passing events that you don't have to assign meaning to or do anything with.

- Set a time later in the day for thinking/worrying if you think you may need to do something with the thought. The self-coaching may sound like "I can't focus on this right now, but from 7 to 7:15 this evening I'll investigate this thought again and see if I need to do anything with it." MCT author Pia Callesen refers to this as holding gum in your mouth but not chewing it until the designated time pops up. You will likely find that after a while, you don't need your scheduled worry time anymore. Or at least you need less and less of it.

- Remember the point isn't to feel better (you will once you get the hang of it, but we have to do some serious retraining of the habit formation pathways of the brain first). Don't think of continued distress as a failure of the technique. Remember that thought control isn't the point, reducing thought engagement is. That's it. That's the trick. You got this.

Prayer and Meditation

These are the things that people tell me over and over are their two biggest coping skills. You may be rolling your eyes up in your head at me over this one, I know. Prayer? I don't do religion. Meditate? I sure as hell don't have time to sit and "ommmm" for an hour. NEXT SKILL PLEASE!

But let's unpack these skills before you decide they're not for you. You want to be able to be fully informed before telling me to fuck off, right?

The reason that both prayer and meditation feel weird and icky for people is that they are tied, intrinsically, to spirituality. And so many people have had really fucked-up experiences with one of the common expressions of spirituality . . . organized religion. Even though I was raised by theological scholars who encouraged healthy skepticism of bullshit coupled with a doctrine of inclusivity and acceptance, I still had plenty of churchgoing experiences that left me angry, sad, and disconnected. After all, my parents were fighting against a huge tsunami of religion as a mechanism of toxic control, rather than an impetus for love, care, and action. And while I wasn't anti-religion, I wasn't sure where I fit into some sort of religious practice.

Then spirituality (and, to some extent, the organization of spirituality into religious practice) came up over and over and OVER again in my dissertation research. I couldn't hide from my own damn data. And while trying to come up with a way to categorize how we think about and use spirituality and religion in our lives, I bumped into Geral Blanchard's definition of spirituality. He keeps it simple, and simple is what I needed: Spirituality is just *purposeful belonging*.

Our fundamental mechanisms of invoking this purposeful belonging are prayer and meditation. I know this still sounds very incense, chanting, and woo-woo . . . but I've had several people tell me since my coping skills zine (which this book draws from) first came out that they had a huge shift in their thinking thanks to how I presented my understanding of prayer and meditation.

Essentially, what we have agreed, culturally, to define as prayer is just *talking to*. Speaking either to ourselves or to something bigger than ourselves (God, YHWH, Higher Power, or whomever you speak to) about our wants, needs, desires, and intentions. Human beings are storytellers, after all. We even tell ourselves stories in our sleep, though we call it dreaming. Talking through our situation in this manner can be far more powerful than talking to a friend, family member, or therapist. It's a grounding experience that helps us be more aware of our thoughts, feelings, and behaviors.

So what's mindful meditation, then? Meditation is *listening to*. Meditation is the process of quieting ourselves down enough to hear what's going on inside us. Our minds are brilliant at creating endless amounts of chatter that we often talk back to without listening first. Meditation doesn't require a red cushion, a saffron robe, and a shaved head (unless that works for you). It just means a willingness to hear yourself before you start arguing back.

And while prayer is deeply unique and personal and I wouldn't feel comfortable giving anyone prayer instructions, I not only have a longtime meditation practice, I'm also officially trained as a meditation instructor. So I can offer some suggestions in that regard.

Mindfulness and Meditation

Mindfulness is the basic human ability to be aware and fully present in our own lives, to bear witness to the workings of our body and mind as well as what is going on around us. Jon Kabat-Zinn, likely the best-known mindfulness instructor in the Western world, states that mindfulness is just *awareness*. It is the natural state of the human body, especially when we are young, but it is something we become trained out of when we developmentally get to the place where we realize we can escape our present reality and be somewhere else. In fact, we do that so often researchers have found that at least half of our waking hours are spent with wandering minds.

Mindfulness does not require meditation. Mindfulness is essentially the best path we have figured out for accepting the is-ness of our lives. This isn't to say that we should take shit lying down; it's about recognizing the reality of the current moment rather than getting so wrapped up in how we want it to be or how it should be that we get stuck. When we get stuck in how things should be, we get stuck in unceasing judgement, which is not a place systemic change comes from.

Meditation, by contrast, is a formal process of focused attention and does not have to include mindfulness. Mindfulness meditation is where the two meet. This is where that process of awareness is brought into the formal practice of focused attention. This doesn't mean perfect attention, but it is a process of recognizing when the mind wanders and refocusing awareness back to the present when it does, usually with some kind of anchor (the breath is the most common).

There is not a "correct" form of mindfulness, meditation, or mindfulness meditation. They all have the same goal of helping achieve a peaceful mind and manage stress, so I am including a wide variety of practices for you to experiment with.

This Is Your Brain on Mindfulness and Meditation

Mindfulness has been so well researched at this point, the research-backed benefits would be an encyclopedia in and of themselves. But here are a few of the big ones.

Mindfulness has been found to:

- Positively impact overall human functioning (cognitions, emotions, physiology, and behavior)

- Improve attention and focus

- Provide greater empathy and compassion, positively impacting interpersonal behavior

- Reduce proactive interference (when old stuff we know gets in the way of new stuff we are trying to learn)

- Help manage caregiver burnout

- Help manage chronic pain (showing just as much benefit as CBT)

- Help overcome insomnia

- Help with the management of mental health issues, including depression, anxiety, and PTSD

- Increase the body's immune response

A lot of studies have been done specifically about meditation, and the results are fascinating. We have literally thousands of years of mindfulness and meditation practice documented in human history that include reported benefits of the practices. With the advent of fMRI (functional magnetic resonance imaging), we can actually *see* how mindfulness and meditation affect the functioning and even the neuroplasticity of the brain, which is the brain's ability to grow, learn, and heal damage.

Let's go back to the idea of a vagal window of tolerance. More and more research is demonstrating that meditation not only helps in the moment, but also helps us remain in our window of tolerance in general, not just when we are meditating, by creating positive alternations in the neural activity and connectivity of the default mode networks of the brain (the storytelling brain). This means meditation is teaching the brain to learn process-specific states of calm (all-the-time regulation) instead of state-specific calm (meaning we're calm when we meditate).

Trauma-Sensitive Practice

While mindfulness and meditation can be of huge benefit to a large number of people, they aren't magic for everyone, and they may require trauma-sensitive modifications, just like any body-oriented practice. If you have a trauma history and try to sit down to meditate following any standard instructions, it's possible that it will fuck you up.

Things you may notice that are signs of dorsal and ventral vagal responses that may be associated with trauma (either fight and flight activation or freezing up) can include:

- Prolonged, uncontrollable crying

- Shortness of breath

- Trembling

- Clenched fists

- Getting very pale or very flushed

- Excessive sweating

- Depersonalization

- Derealization

- Fear

- Panic

Having a trauma history, or having a trauma response while meditating, doesn't mean you can't meditate or practice mindfulness. But those of us with intense trauma histories need to have space for *choice*. This means choice in working through a trauma history in our own time and in our own way, instead of having memories flood our present moment and disrupt our lives. Traditional meditation practices encourage us to go back to the breath and to treat any triggers or activation as thinking that detracts from the present moment. Instead, a trauma-informed practice helps us lean into uncomfortable feelings without losing our zone of tolerance.

If trauma is an issue for you, here are some tips, many of them inspired by David Treleaven's book *Trauma-Sensitive Mindfulness*.

1. Recognize your internal *go* and *stop* signals (thoughts, feelings, body sensations). You don't have to sit and stew in emotional pain. Some discomfort can help us grow, but retraumatizing ourselves fixes fucking nothing. Notice which practices are helpful and which are activating. Get up and take a break when you need to, but next time stay seated just a little longer.

2. You don't have to sit in physical pain either. Take breaks when you need to or alter how you are holding your body. Move into a more comfortable position or wiggle in place a little. While meditation (specifically mindfulness meditation) has been shown in research to be incredibly helpful to pain management, it's not supposed to be torture. Support your body in whatever ways you need to to be as comfortable as possible.

3. Meditation exercises often suggest closing your eyes. This is totally optional. If you don't feel comfortable with your eyes closed in the environment you're in, leave them open. Or start with a soft gaze as a step towards closing your eyes.

4. If your practice involves attending a class, talk to the teacher. If there is any hands-on component (like if your practice involves yoga or tai chi), you can tell them not

to provide physical adjustments (meaning, not to touch you).

Just like with everything else regarding *your* mental and physical health, listen to your body more than you listen to me. Don't do things that are awful and upsetting for you. Meditation is a chance to work through crap without being overactivated. So if you are overactivated by something, it may not be for you, at least not right now.

Basic Mindfulness Meditation Instructions

This is the classic, go-to mindfulness-based meditation that uses breath as the anchor to the present moment.

- Settle in a comfortable position. Sitting with an aligned back is the classic method (either on a cushion or in a straight-backed chair), but if that isn't a position you can get into or maintain, no worries—settle your body to be as presence-focused as possible.

- Bring your awareness to the physical sensations of your body. Where do you feel the pressure of your body making contact with your chair, bed, or floor? What other sensations (like air, temperature, texture) do you notice? Spend a minute or two noticing those sensations.

- Now bring your awareness to your lower abdomen, recognizing the sensations of your breath moving in and out of your body. You can place a hand on your abdomen to help you feel the sensation if you are struggling to make that connection. Notice your abdominal wall stretching and inflating with each in-breath and gently deflating with each out-breath.

- Continue to follow the breath in and out, giving yourself permission to just be in the experience of your breath.

- Eventually (probably sooner rather than later) you will notice that your mind is wandering. You start daydreaming, planning, getting consumed with other thoughts. My brain likes to sing songs and make shopping lists, personally. This is what brains do. It doesn't make you a mindful-meditation failure. Just when you notice that you're doing it, label it "thinking" and focus back on the breath.

- Bring curiosity and patience to your wanderings, rather than frustration. Notice what was going on and return to the breath.

Most research demonstrates that 15 minutes of practice is the amount of time it takes to gain the benefits of mindfulness meditation. If you can't tolerate it for that long, that's also OK. Practice working up to it. If you find that it's helpful and want to extend time out further that's also great, but not required.

Mindfully Eating a Raisin

This mindful eating practice is a classic MBSR (mindfulness-based stress reduction) technique. It gives you a different element to focus on, other than your breath.

- Place a few raisins in your hand. And no you don't have to use raisins, any food will do. I've found that even people who don't like raisins are not bothered by them in this exercise. But if they really gross you out, grab something else.

- Pretend this is your first day on the planet. This is a new food that you have never seen before, and you are an alien explorer that is going to make scientific study of raisins and raisin-ness. Use all five of your senses to explore it. Turn it around with your fingers, notice the color, the tactical sensations. How does it fold or reflect light? What does it smell like when you hold it up to your nose? Does it make any sound if you apply pressure?

- You will start having thoughts of the "Why am I doing this? This is fucking weird" variety. Totally normal. Just recognize them as thoughts you are having and bring yourself back to the activity.

- Bring the object slowly to your mouth. Notice how automatic it is for your hand to bring nourishment up to your mouth. Notice whatever anticipation you are experiencing. Is your mouth watering? Gently place the raisin on your tongue without biting down. Explore the sensation of the raisin in your mouth.

- When you are ready, bite down. Notice the taste that is released when you do so. Notice how you habitually move it to one side of your mouth over the other. Slowly chew the raisin. Notice how it changes in texture and flavor as you chew. When you feel ready to swallow, notice your conscious intention to do so. Pay attention to the sensation of it moving down your throat, to your esophagus.

How did the experience of eating differ when you did so mindfully? What did you notice? What did you enjoy? What was uncomfortable?

Non-Mindfulness Meditation

There are lots of other forms of meditation besides mindfulness. So if mindfulness isn't your jam, or you just want to add some other kinds of meditation to your toolkit, here are a couple ideas.

Mantra Meditation

Using a mantra to meditate is the best-known form of meditation that isn't mindfulness based. Mantras are used as a tool to free the mind (or to be freed from the mind). They help break the cycle of spinning thoughts that lead to anxiety, self-doubt, and the like.

Mantras actually soothe the default mode of the brain, keeping it from going into storytelling mode and creating anxious thoughts.

You can chant any contemplative expression from your faith system (like "Hail Mary, full of grace") or something more generally spiritual (like "I am Divine Love"), or any secular humanist phrase, and gain the same default-mode benefit. Or maybe there is a certain mantra about your path of healing that you want to use.

Once you've decided on a mantra, find your comfy place and set a timer for yourself. Start with a few deep breaths and then start changing your mantra (in your head is fine, out-loud voice is also fine). If you catch your thoughts wandering, bring them back to the mantra.

Meditation in Motion

What we often refer to as "walking meditation" is really just "meditation in motion." Whatever device you may use for mobility will become part of the process.

- Find an unobstructed space in which you can move back and forth in a reasonably straight line for about 10 feet (yes, you can also do a greater distance). If you are walking and are able to do so barefoot (and it's an area that is safe for you to be barefoot), you may find this helpful to gain more awareness of how your body creates balance for movement.

- If you are walking, bring your attention to your feet, shifting your weight from side to side and front to back, as far as you are able to do so comfortably. Lift your head and chest so you are facing forward, let your shoulders drop away from your ears. You can clasp your hands behind your back, hold them in front of you, or let them hang loosely at your sides.

- If you're comfortably able, lift up one of your legs. It doesn't matter which, but take notice. Pay attention to how your weight shifts in your body when you do so. What does the other side of your body need to do to hold your full weight? Move your lifted foot forward, then place your heel on the ground and roll the rest of your foot down, ending with your toes. Pay attention to how your other foot begins to lift and move forward as well. Bring that foot forward and repeat.

- If you use a device for mobility, focus your attention on the sensations of movement. For example, if you use your hands to connect to the mobility support and guide you forward, connect with that sensation. Feel the sensation of moving forward and your connection to being embodied and supported in that experience. If you are using a chair that relies on voice, facial expression identification, or the like, focus on how you engage your body and connect to the chair to create movement. What shifts do you feel physically and energetically?

- No matter how you create movement, your mind will wander as minds like to do. As your attention wanders off, you can bring yourself back to present practice with the thought of "attention engagement forward" or an anchoring reminder of your choice.

- When you come to the end of your path (unless it was a circle to begin with), turn fully around, face the direction from which you came, and start over. If you are moving in a circular shape, simply notice that you have completed one full round.

Escapism

If prayer and meditation are ways of being in the present moment, escapism is a way of pulling back from an untenable situation without getting muddled up in the past. OK, what's the difference, fancy doctor lady? *Escapism* is a conscious move into another world for a while. It could be through guided imagery, a wonderful book, moving music, or binge-watching *Grace and Frankie* on Netflix.

Escapism is intentionally moving to another space in a mental and emotional way (but of course you may go all balls out and take a vacay . . . that works too). It gives you a chance to soothe your tired self without getting trapped in a nasty cycle of perseverating on memories. Seriously. Go to the thrift store and buy up all the Baby-Sitters Club books (or whatever you loved to read as a kid), run a bubble bath, and escape the fuck up outta this mess.

The important thing is that the escapism be proactive rather than passive. A lot of people who struggle with depression report spending a ton of time sitting around and watching TV . . . and report that they don't feel any better for doing so. To use terms borrowed from cognitive behavioral therapy, we are looking for things that provide a sense of pleasure and maybe even mastery.

One of the escapism ideas I talked about above is guided imagery. I've found that people get confused about guided imagery and meditation, thinking they are essentially the same thing. In fact, guided imagery is pretty much the opposite of meditation but still a very positive coping skill. Guided imagery is a form of storytelling. It is the use of words (and sometimes music and other soothing sounds) to guide you to a calm, focused, and relaxed state. Oftentimes you're encouraged to use your imagination to picture yourself somewhere calming, like on a beach or in the woods. It's a form of intentional and healthy distraction (escapism) from your current stressful situation.

If you are ruminating and upset and worried for the future (the clinical term is anticipatory distress), then guided imagery helps you refocus your imagination to something that is calming and positive.

Research demonstrates that guided imagery, if done properly, calms our flooding of stress hormones (therefore our emotional turmoil) and helps us manage physical pain by activating our subconscious processes as well as our conscious ones. "Properly" means including the following elements identified by licensed social worker Belleruth Naparstek, one of the first people to utilize guided imagery as a clinical intervention. Her categories, with my brief interpretation of each, are listed below.

- *The Mind-Body Connection:* Guided imagery puts the entirety of your body into the image. The subconscious only understands the present tense, and will relate to sensory cues. Things that help you feel, hear, see, smell, and taste will activate all the right "pay attention" cues in us.

- *The Altered State:* By engaging our entire body in guided imagery we are essentially invoking a form of self-hypnosis. This focused state helps us connect to our creativity and intuition while managing our negative thoughts and feelings. Our brain waves literally change our heartbeat, our breathing patterns, etc.

- *Locus of Control:* Good guided imagery puts YOU in charge of the action. You are being guided, but you are the one doing the real movement in your mind and it is toward a direction that serves your healing and growth.

Belleruth's website, HealthJourneys.com, has a ton of guided imagery audio files that follow these principles. There are also lots of great guided imagery sessions on YouTube and other places on the web. Check some out, keeping in mind the healing elements mentioned above!

Self-Compassion

OK, let's be honest. It's just us here, after all, right? How do you talk to yourself when you fuck up or even think you might have fucked up or that you might fuck up in the future? What kind of nasty things do you say? What tends to trigger that experience for you? How well do you connect to others after shitting all over yourself? Kristin Neff (author of the literal book on self-compassion) says: "If you are continually judging and criticizing yourself while trying to be kind to others, you are drawing artificial boundaries and distinctions that only lead to feelings of separation and isolation."

Instead, treat yourself like you would your best friend. What if they had fucked up hardcore? You would be compassionate, wouldn't you? You wouldn't let them off the hook, but you would help them take responsibility, try to fix the mess they made, and remind them that they are a human being, after all. And human beings fail.

Give yourself the same compassion you would give someone you love. Instead of "I can't believe that bullshit you pulled, why on earth are you even on this planet?????" try "Wow, OK, so that didn't work out. Everything went sideways. I need to figure out the best thing to do now to try to fix as much as possible. And figure out why it went sideways so I can try to avoid it happening again. I feel like shit right now, but I can learn from this and fail differently and fail better next time."

Give Yourself Five Minutes to Channel Your Inner Veruca Salt

Veruca Salt is the horrible child from *Charlie and the Chocolate Factory*. Remember her? Demanding that all eyes be on her and that she get all that she wishes, Veruca gets in the way of what really matters because she takes over.

Anxiety can become the emotional equivalent of Veruca Salt, taking over everything. And sometimes the best way to treat it is to give in. The official therapeutic term for this is *paradoxical intention*.

The idea behind paradoxical intention is that *what you resist persists*. And if you intentionally invoke what is causing you so much anxiety, it loses its power. I like to set a time limit, which helps you know there is something to pull you back from the anxiety pit you are entering. Five minutes to do NOTHING but think of the thing causing anxiety. Nothing else. Just be anxious. But as opposed to being a total bitch like Veruca (and ending up falling down a garbage chute), approach what you are feeling with acceptance. And curiosity. And neutrality. It's just what you feel, right? Not good or bad. And those emotions may be relaying some important information to you, if you open yourself up to really listening to yourself.

And if it's just useless mental jibber-jabber, that's OK, too. I've found I'm really over myself and my bullshit after about three minutes.

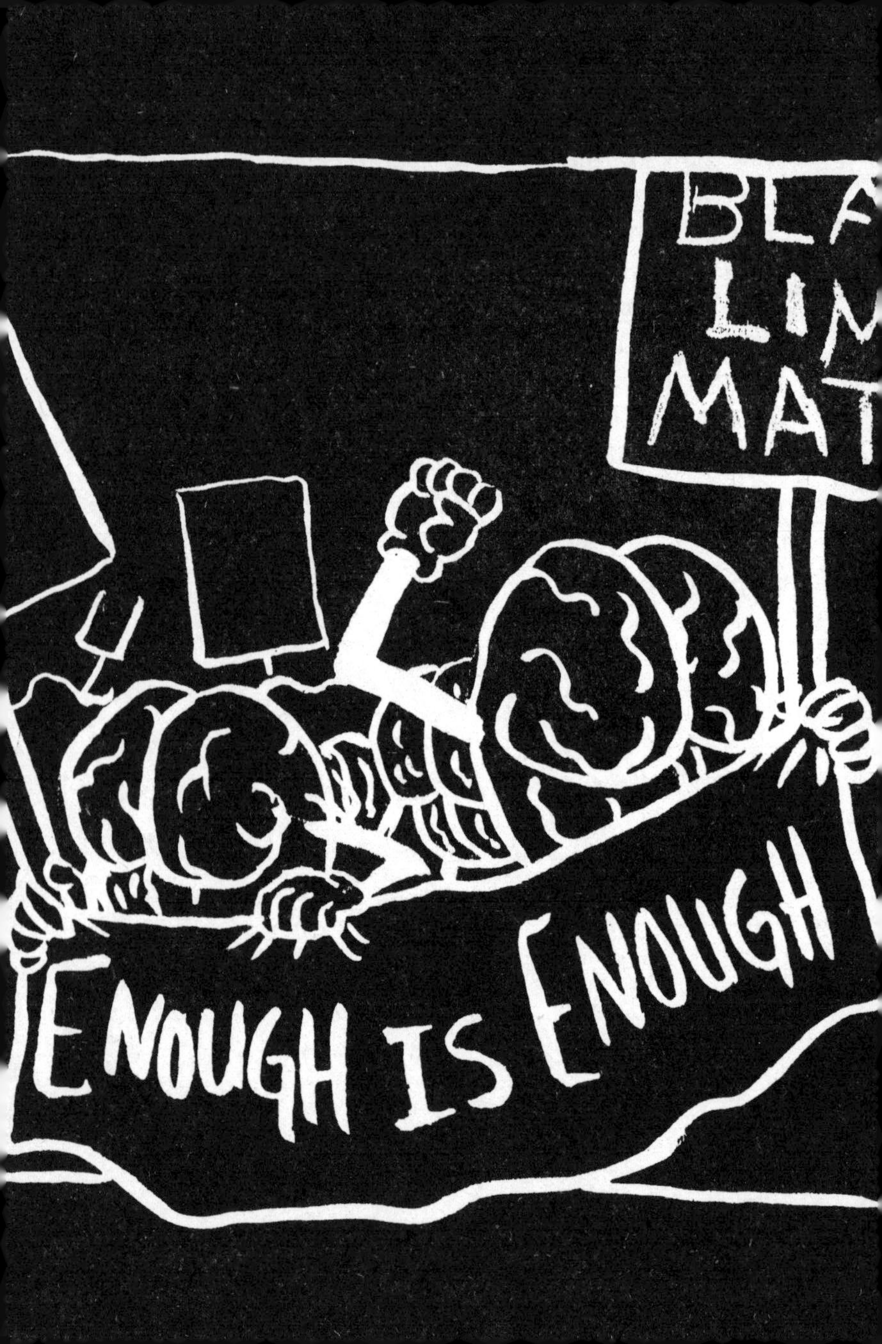
ENOUGH IS ENOUGH

CHAPTER 7: *MITIGATE THE BULLSHIT*: SHIFTING YOUR BEHAVIORS

So now that we've got some tools in our toolbox for mitigating distress by working with our feeling-thoughts, what about shifting our behaviors? This chapter is all about behavioral coping skills: the practical things you can do to manage and tolerate whatever shit is going on. Not by managing your own internal processes, but by better managing whatever it is that you are squaring off against. But do it productively. Don't put in an Uber Eats order for donuts just yet. We're going for pragmatic action plans that help you boss through fucked-up situations.

The Julia Cameron Spot-Check Inventory

The spot-check inventory delineated by Julia Cameron in her book *The Listening Path: The Creative Art of Attention* is an incredibly valuable tool. The concept of being proactive instead of reactive means creating some structure around your thinking process so you can get as clear as possible before doing something. I found this tool so useful I included it as a business strategy in *Unfuck Your Business*, which I co-authored with my publisher, Joe Biel.

Julia recommends asking yourself (and answering for yourself) the five following questions:

1. What do I need to know?

2. What do I need to accept?

3. What do I need to try?

4. What do I need to grieve?

5. What do I need to celebrate?

And yes, really answer all five if you are looking to move the needle. Question 4 helps you release whatever you need to release in order to do the first three things. And question 5 reminds you to pay attention to your progress and successes, which our brains are wired to ignore in favor of the negative.

If this is a helpful tool, and you'd like one that is slightly more in depth in parsing out what you need to do to problem solve? Check out below.

Clarification Exercise: What Problem Are You Trying to Solve?

Are you bumped up against an unsolvable problem? Maybe the issue is the problem itself, not your inability to find a solution. Consider the case of the non–morning person. No matter how many alarms he sets, he can't get up on time. If he could just find that one, loud alarm clock that he could hang up out of reach to ensure he gets to work by 8 a.m. Except maybe the real problem that needs to be solved is why is he not getting enough rest? Is he getting to bed early enough? How is his quality of sleep? Does he have sleep apnea so he is perpetually exhausted? The problem to be solved is not the alarm clock. The problem is the lack of adequate rest.

The media pushback against the marketing of "Lady Doritos" is another good example. The company got huge backlash for saying that women don't like chips that are loud, messy, and hard to carry. Women everywhere banded together with a unified message of "lol, fuck off." Gender differences in chip consumption were not a problem to be solved. Creating an alternate product that all people could use to assist in portability for meals and snacks on the go was what needed to happen to solve the real problem. And the exact same snack, marketed thusly, may have done fantastically well. (Though, for the record, the crumbs at the bottom are always my favorite . . . and I wouldn't want anything that didn't have them.)

So when trying to manage some life bullshittery, check in to make sure you are solving the right problem before you get started on the solving part. I mean seriously, did we really need Lady Doritos? I call it looking at the problem with sideways eyes. Literally shift your perspective and ask others for theirs. Some super fancy tips:

1. Ask yourself: Is your current problem unsolvable? If so, time to stop perseverating on trying to solve it!

2. Have you tried solving a different problem yet? Something that might get you to a more manageable place, that's related to this scenario but has a different focus? If no, let's try that!

3. If you can, collect yourself one other person. Maybe two. Not a group. Because this could lead to a descent into group chaos or distraction. Look for people you trust and respect but who have a different worldview than you. Different perspectives are helpful.

4. Ask questions. Literally just ask questions. No solution offering or suggestions. Just questions associated with your situation.

5. And collect them and write them down.

6. Review your questions. Sort them into categories based on your emerging themes. What sort of categories are taking shape? Can any of these categories be distilled down into fewer questions? Maybe one singular question?

7. Do any of these questions seem approachable as possibly solvable? Mark those. Circle, highlight, whatever.

8. Any emerging themes again? Anything that can be distilled down into fewer questions or a singular question?

9. Ask for feedback from others if you can. Even if no one participated in the process up until this point. What do they notice? Do they see anything missing, question-wise?

10. From the solvable list, pick a question you are ready to tackle. Dump out what you were trying to resolve and focus on this one instead. NOW brainstorm ideas for resolution.

Building Structure Within Chaos: Create Your Ladder

When your ability to manage huge, incoming waves of bullshit is compromised for WHATEVER reason, this is a fantastic technique for getting through days and weeks of really stressful times. Maybe you are dealing with a chronic health condition (whether physical, mental, or both). Maybe you are newly in recovery. Maybe you are just going through a truly awful period in your life with significant, shitty changes.

And hell, even if you have good change going on, it can still be intensely stressful. Maybe you're moving, going back to school, getting a promotion, getting married, or having a baby. It seems shitty and unfair to compare it to someone going through cancer treatment and it's definitely not near as bad. But higher levels of stress for any reason mean coping skill activation time.

Building a system of self-care strategies (I mean, aren't those coping skills, too??) that help you mitigate ongoing stress can really help you get through the type of issue that is more marathon than sprint. We've read articles (or seen on Insta) tributes along the lines of "a good skin care routine will totally change your life!" I mean, not in and of itself. That's bypassing the depth of how fucked up shit can be. No one has loved me less because I had a zit on my chin. And not having a zit didn't make a shitty boss less shitty.

But. BUT. Self-care strategies can build on each other in a way that helps support your ability to cope. Think of each of your self-care strategies as rungs on a ladder. You are climbing this ladder out of stress and overwhelm into stability. Think about what a quality daily routine looks like for you, and list strategies in the sequential order that works best for you. For example, some people feel best when they shower first thing. My husband likes to shower later in the day, after he has done grubby work like dishes, or yard work, or cat boxes. Makes total sense, right? They may not be empirically important but they are important to YOUR day. Maybe your routine includes a butter coffee and puppy snuggles. It's your list, so you define what's important.

The great thing about this image is you will really pay attention to how important all of these activities are to your well-being because each one is a step up and out. If you miss a rung, you feel the difference in your balance immediately. The next step is that much harder to take. And if you start pulling out lots of rungs willy-nilly? You are either hanging on for dear life with no real movement upward, *or you are going to fall*.

Time Management

Stress experts talk a ton about time management, which may or may not relate to you. I know plenty of people are brilliant at time management and also completely stressed out because time is still finite. But for some of us, the overwhelm diminishes our sense of time and increases to the point that the idea of managing anything seems impossible. I first wrote about the following technique some years ago and noticed it had gotten popular again after several years of Covid feral-ness for people who needed some kind of system to work on projects. If your overwhelm is making it difficult for you to focus on longer-term projects, this may be a helpful strategy.

The entrepreneur Francesco Cirillo created the Pomodoro Technique as a method of task management in the face of overwhelment. It's easy AF, y'all. The pomodoro in question is the little kitchen timer that looks like a tomato. You've totally seen it before. You break down whatever bullshittery you have to tackle into chunks of time that are manageable for an adult attention span with breaks added in for relief. You set your timer for 25 minutes and work. Then you take a 5-minute break. After four Pomodoro cycles, you take a longer break.

You start training yourself into better focus, concentration, and time management by working in sprints rather than marathons, with built-in breaks to help you maintain motivation. It doesn't make completely impossible goals suddenly magically attainable, but it CAN help you keep from mind-fucking yourself into thinking that you won't finish something that is actually pretty doable. If nothing else, it's a really good system for giving something your best shot so you can be proud you were proactive and tried your damn ass off.

Planning Your Life to Support Your Best Self (Chaos Goblin or Otherwise)

I am saying this with all the love in my heart a fellow chaos goblin can provide. Managing my time/energy/resources effectively didn't really work until I got honest with myself about who I really am, not who I want to be. I will never have an Insta-inspo life. I don't even use an insta-pot, ffs . . . I'm still stuck on the crockpots I grew up with.

Managing my time and my priorities works way better when I own that, while it's not fun, I do better when I get up early rather than stay up late. And when I exercise a little each morning, although I find it rude how much just going for a walk helps everything else. I have far fewer migraines and far less chronic pain in general, and I say that as someone who is already really active, teaches yoga, etc. My body needs to be on an earlier schedule instead of a later one and start with movement. Ugh, OK, fine.

I keep snacks pretty much everywhere so if I am hungry, I won't eat something that my body has already told me will cause a problem for which it will punish me. Even though I love to cook, sometimes I need access to something quickly, so I always have a few good frozen meal options, as well as snackable things like dairy-free ice cream sandwiches, popcorn, my favorite Siete chips, etc.

My house is designed around my comfort, not aesthetics, though I think it's aesthetically fun, too. Besides being prepared for all snaccidents, I keep comfortable blankets and pillows everywhere, books and magazines in all the places I like to read, etc. Doing things like moving my supplements to my bedside table has made it far easier to take them when I am supposed to. Keeping a pair of fingernail clippers pretty much everywhere keeps me from picking at ragged cuticles. Basically everything is organized in ways that make sense to me and make it easier to put my hands on it when I need it. My niblings know where their stuff is in the house if they swing by and I'm not there. My clients know where everything is in the back offices in the same way.

Marie Kondo or Martha Stewart would probably weep at all of it, but it all works for me and that's the important thing. And it does help my stress levels in small-but-impactful-over-time ways. Because if I'm already having a crap week but then forget to take my magnesium, or I'm already having a crap week but don't have anything healthy-ish to eat, or any number of small things that chip away at me being my best self? I slide into stress-monster mode far too quickly.

So when it comes to mitigating the bullshit, this is one of the most important tasks. Think about how you actually live your life and what things truly help you live it in the best possible manner. If making the bed in the morning is a fantastic habit for you because coming home to a made bed helps you feel calm and cared for? Do the thing. If you don't give a shit about the unmade bed, spend that time doing something else that is helpful instead. A perfectly pulled espresso, an acai bowl, a few minutes of stretching, or a few minutes of watching cartoons.

No judgements on my end . . . the point is to create a life that is as supportive of your best self as possible.

Saying No to Things

Y'all? The word "no" though? Scariest word in the human language. Probably because it is the most powerful. Saying no to things that we don't want to do is hard enough. Saying no to things we really would like to do is far more difficult. And? Oftentimes far more important. Saying no to things means thinking about the ultimate cost of our decisions and planning accordingly.

And please understand, I'm not saying don't do things that will cost you later . . . I'm saying take those costs into account in your decision-making process. Going out with friends in the middle of a pain flare may fill your connection cup enough that it is well worth having more pain the next day. But also maybe not. And this is about planning mindfully and skillfully. You would (I hope) check the weather before setting out on a day hike. And we should do the same thing with other activities and plans.

Have Some Fun, FFS

We need to laugh. We NEED to laugh, y'all.

Laughing is good for us emotionally, right? It decreases stress hormones in the body and helps us think more creatively. Did you know it has direct physical benefits as well? Like immediate benefits, not just the reducing of wear and tear on the body by reducing stress hormones. It also relaxes our muscles, strengthens our heart and lungs, and decreases physical pain.

Be an epic goofball. Seriously. Praise be any new fad that gets people out and doing stuff again. Remember a few years ago, for about five minutes, Pokémon Go was beating out porn in internet usage? That's crazy awesome. Who knows what the fuck the new hot thing will be by the time you are reading this book, but I am all in for anything that gives us permission to be epic goofballs. I will talk in a crazy accent, wear weird t-shirts (I love buying t-shirts from the boys' section of the store) to work (the benefit of being self-employed . . . I set the dress code), dance with my waiter in the middle of the restaurant (thanks, Paul!), and have my husband (a deeply patient man) push me through the grocery store parking lot while I stand on the shopping cart.

Because sometimes we just *need* to laugh. Taking a minute to step out of everything heavy and remember that life can also be enjoyable gives us the perspective and energy we need to fight another day.

CHAPTER 8: COPING WITH BURNOUT, IMPOSTER SYNDROME, AND SELF-SABOTAGE

*O*K, lady, all well and good with your coping skills, but some aspects of stress are more complex than others. Some of the main "what-abouts" that I run into around stress topics involve the complexity of burnout, imposter syndrome, and self-sabotage behaviors. So it would be shitty to not cover these topics. And I don't aim to be shitty, so let's get into it.

Stress and Burnout

To be human is to burn the fuck out. Burnout is by no means a new, modern ailment. The concept of burnout has existed throughout literature (from the Old Testament to Shakespeare) and has been scientifically studied enough to be operationalized. Meaning, researchers took a big and vague concept and were able to measure and define and make sense of it in as science-y a way as possible.

Meaning it's not just an "Oh, you seem super tired right now, why don't you take a personal day?" Burnout is a complex physiological and psychological response to stressful events.

But what is burnout exactly? Let's start with how the World Health Organization defines it: a syndrome "resulting from chronic workplace stress that has not been successfully managed."

First off, that's vague and victim-blamey. Second, it doesn't operationalize what stress is (so we are gonna do that, too).

Finally, it frames burnout as a workplace-specific phenomenon. This is probably because all the research around burnout is workplace-centered, which I feel ought not to be the case. Stress exists in all life domains. So if burnout is a response to stress, it doesn't take a huge leap of logic to recognize that it can exist in any part of our lives. Hopefully the Covid-19 pandemic years have made that apparent and burnout research will start to expand past workplace scenarios and reflect that.

A lot of people had to quickly convert their home lives to being their everything lives in 2020. They didn't always lose their jobs, but they had to find ways to do them from home. Their kids moved to video-based school and it wasn't great but it was . . . manageable. At first. And then weeks became months became years. Things could have been so much worse, absolutely. And both perspective and gratitude are important.

But? We experienced losses both tangible and intangible. There were moments of big, spiky grief. And then there was this more nebulous, continuous stream of grief and loss and bereavement of our former lives as we continued to try to create some level of new normal. And there is only so much of that that anyone can take.

Everyone responds to events based on how we evaluate them. How we evaluate them is based on our past histories, our past success in handling stressful situations, our available resources, our perceptions of how other people are handling things in the past and present, etc. And holy hell, this was too much for anyone to sustain for as long as we all did without some emotional damage.

But that begs an interesting question. What is the nature of that emotional damage? We were calling it burnout, but were we putting a new term on an old problem?

When a more complex model of burnout than just "really fucking tired" emerged from research, the question became: Is burnout really just depression wearing different pants? Burnout and depression do share some features (loss of interest, impaired concentration). Or since stress can lead to anxiety, we might ask: Is burnout just anxiety wearing a new and interesting hat? Basically, researchers wanted to know if we are renaming a condition we already know about and therefore not providing people with the appropriate treatment options they really need.

Singular studies comparing burnout with depression and anxiety showed mixed results. So a couple researchers bundled up all these studies and ran something known as a meta analysis, which is just when someone combines the data from a multitude of scientific studies addressing the same question in order to get an overall answer to what each individual study was trying to figure out.

And short answer? Burnout, anxiety, and depression are all their own unique constructs. Burnout isn't depression or anxiety being misnamed. Which means you may also be experiencing depression or anxiety (or both, lucky you). Or you may be experiencing "just" burnout. And medications for depression or anxiety won't support you feeling better.

Burnout isn't nebulous and undefinable, it is a predictor of many physical diseases, just like many other mental health conditions. This is most likely related to the chronic-stress component of it. It's been correlated with headaches, chronic fatigue, gastrointestinal issues, sleep issues, and more frequent colds and flus, as well as increasingly serious issues like substance abuse, coronary heart disease, respiratory illness, and overall early mortality. Which means we should take it as seriously as we would any other medical condition.

The Elements of Burnout

So let's dig deeper into what burnout is. As mentioned earlier, burnout has appeared throughout literature as a common human condition. But it usually was only referred to as the emotional exhaustion that comes with constant stress becoming continuing distress.

One of the names you will see associated most with burnout research is that of social psychologist Christina Maslach. Social psychologists focus on how people operate within society. Therefore, Dr. Maslach suspected that burnout was more than just our experience of exhaustion and was also about how our internal world affects and is affected by our social systems. That is, burnout only exists in a social context. It isn't purely individual. Her research on the construct found that three distinct components emerged: emotional exhaustion, feelings of cynicism, and reduced personal accomplishment.

Emotional Exhaustion: This is the part we all think of when we think of burnout. The feeling of being emotionally overextended and depleted of emotional resources. It's when we feel drained all the time, with no space for replenishment. We feel overloaded and in conflict with most everyone around us. This is considered the individual stress dimension of burnout.

Cynicism: This is when our responses to those around us become detached, cynical, or negative. It develops as a buffer against the constant experience of emotional exhaustion. We're feeling raw and overwhelmed, so we emotionally check out. We end up disconnected from and sometimes even dehumanizing those around us. This is considered the interpersonal dimension of burnout.

Reduced Personal Accomplishment: This is our sense of not being as competent or accomplished in our tasks. Because the burnout model is specifically about work, this is what is being referenced . . . but I think it easily extends to other life domains, because no area of life is task-free and doesn't have people who rely on us. Whether or not our ability to do a good or adequate job has actually been impeded, our internal report card is one of failure. Which is why this is considered the self-evaluation dimension of burnout.

Early research presumed that the emotional exhaustion element kicked in first, in response to high demands and overload, which would lead to a negative interpersonal appraisal, which then would lead to feelings of inadequacy and failure. It may not be so cleanly sequential in reality (life is messy in reality), but it makes sense that physiological exhaustion leads to emotional exhaustion, which becomes the main tipping point for the other relational changes that then take place.

Well That All Fucking Sucks, What's the Solution?

Once the components of burnout had been operationalized, the next task of social psychologists was to figure out what the opposite of burnout was. Researchers ended up settling on a construct they termed "engagement." Engagement (in this case) refers not to tasting wedding cake flavors and putting a deposit on a venue, but to a state of being where you consider the time you spend as being productive and fulfilling in the domain you are in. Again, they are studying work. And, again, I'd say this fits in any life domain.

If we were to look for three components of engagement to contrast with the three components of burnout, we would see:

High energy

Strong involvement

A sense of efficacy

These all sound great, right? So how do you get there?

If you google "managing burnout" you are going to get a lot of hits. I got a return of 36,100,000 results. And they were all in the vein of "roll your body in coconut oil and do yoga." No shade to either—I happen to be a yoga teacher, and while I don't roll around in coconut oil (no kinksharming if that's your bag), I do cook with it regularly. In terms of managing burnout, those are individual strategies. Sometimes the only power we have in a situation is the power of our own response. And I appreciate that's sometimes what we have to roll with.

But since I can't hand you a jar of coconut oil and a slip and slide, I'm going to share a therapeutic training technique that has been consistently the most helpful for my clients during the pandemic. It's not an in-the-moment distress tolerance skill, but a learning-to-ride-the-bike skill that takes some practice.

The idea is that when the overwhelm arises, we typically respond in one of two ways: We let it pull us under (understandably so). Or we try to overpower it so we can struggle through (also very understandable).

However, powering through is just as untenable in the long run as giving up. The metaphor I share with my clients is that it's like trying to hold a beach ball underwater. We can use all our time and attention and focus on doing so, but eventually our focus gets distracted for just a second or our arms get a bit tired and the ball pops up and smacks us in the face.

And that brings us back to the reality we were all living in. Remember our discussion of metacognitive therapy in Chapter 6? Well this approach is also really helpful when thinking about burnout. Just as a refresher, researchers have found that MCT techniques are effective at keeping the prefrontal cortex online because they focus on how we are thinking. This is different from cognitive behavioral therapy, which focuses on what we are thinking, with the assumption that our thoughts are wrong. Just like the term "meta" implies, we are going one step up to look at the bigger picture. The idea is that when we are burned out, how we think about a fucked-up situation becomes sticky, making persistent issues with anxiety almost inevitable. That is, we focus on the anxiety because it pops up and our brains start yelling, "This is super important . . . drop everything!"

This technique is designed to be something you practice until it becomes your new cognitive habit, just like going to the gym and working out until you have strength and lung capacity to go hiking without exhausting or injuring yourself. It's adapted from an exercise used by the Metacognitive Therapy Institute, which suggests practicing the technique twice a day for four weeks to build a solid neural pathway for this process. I know this seems like a big time hog of a project, but in reality, you are really only looking at spending 10–15 minutes each practice session.

To do the exercise, first take a seat wherever you like.

Then identify two sounds in your area that are different in loudness and not close to each other. This can be the clock on the wall ticking while you listen to music on your phone or tap on a table.

Spend a few minutes changing your focus of attention between the two, paying attention to both the sounds themselves and the placement of the sounds.

Once you feel comfortable shifting your focus slowly, spend some time shifting back and forth rapidly, again focusing on both the sounds and the placement of the sounds.

Once you have the shifting down, spend a few minutes practicing noticing both at the same time.

If there are other sounds going on in your environment and you're feeling sassy, go ahead and add them to the mix.

The point of this process is to help you notice what's going on in your mind and body, without trying to suppress it or become consumed by it. Thinking is just something brains do that you can recognize, focus more attention on if it's a legitimate worry, or let it hum in the background if your brain is just spinning. As I mentioned earlier, metacognitive therapist and author Pia Callesen uses the analogy of holding gum in your mouth without chewing it. You aren't getting consumed by the emotional overwhelm and you aren't trying to suppress it. You're recognizing it and tucking it away to deal with when you have better time and space and capacity to do so. The more you are able to keep your prefrontal cortex online, the more effective you will be at managing the fuckery being slung your way.

This isn't to say that doing yoga and the like isn't also incredibly effective for burnout, if that is something that really nourishes you. Anything that is supportive of healing your emotional exhaustion is something you should do more of.

Though sometimes doing more actually means doing less. Meaning, doing more nothing. If hitting the gym or the sangha or the dojo or the studio or any of those places is incredibly healing for you, put that in your calendar and treat it like you would any other vital appointment. But if you feel like you "ought" to be doing those things because you saw it on a burnout-prevention listicle somewhere? Fuck it. Have a nice meal and a hot bath and go to bed at a reasonable hour instead. That's also excellent medicine.

The Six Relational Domains of Preventing Burnout

Individual strategies can be helpful in a moment of overwhelm, but the research on burnout has found that social-organizational strategies are ultimately the most effective in combating burnout. Burnout is a relational problem that needs a relational solution.

All of these workers organizing and unionizing make my activist heart explode with joy. Whether you stage a revolution or not, there are many things one can do formally or informally in any environment to combat burnout at a relational (social-organizational) level.

Six key domains have been identified as means of empowering people and preventing and/or treating burnout: workload, control, recognition/reward, community, fairness, and values.

Workload: When a workload is consistently pushed into overload, it is not sustainable or manageable. There isn't time to rest, recover, and restore balance. Instead, our capacity to meet demand becomes depleted and we have no time to refine and enhance existing skills or learn and become effective in new ones. Even in fast-paced environments and busy time periods, expectations can be set that we're human and we are doing the best we can and we are all helping each other out. And that takes off the pressure of going 100 mph until collapse. You can value healthy meals but use a meal-delivery service or pre-prepped ingredients for cooking if you can afford to. You can use the hell out of your crockpot and freeze leftovers for the next week rather than doing fancy gourmet shit every day. You can use compostable plates and cutlery to knock down the time you spend on dishes after. Look at where you are spending a ton of time and see where you can save time without losing out on things that are important to you.

Control: When we lack autonomy and do not have the capacity to influence decision-making processes, we are far more likely to experience burnout. When a task needs to be done, but people are given the flexibility to create a system around how they work rather than being expected to adapt to a system? Game changer. (Like . . . why can't people sit down to be comfortable? Or stand? Or bounce on a bouncy ball? Or write a paper by talk-to-text? Or what-the-fuck-ever gets the job done?)

Recognition/Reward: When our efforts are devalued (either financially, institutionally, or socially) we are far more likely to experience burnout. The fight over a minimum wage increase astonishes me. I don't know why anyone thinks $15 an hour is a lot of money and fast food work is unskilled. That's a rant for another day. In any case, valuing people's labor financially is huge. But people need to be recognized in other non-financial ways as well. That's somewhere we can start immediately. And I don't mean just the "yaaay, pizza party for the crew" kind of way (not turning down pizza, tho . . . dairy-free cheese on mine plz). I mean things like consistently thanking people for how they show the fuck up for us. For being the people we can rely on. The people who have our backs in literal and figurative ways. (But also pay us what we're worth, yakoke.)

Community: When we feel like we don't belong, we experience burnout. We don't quit jobs, we quit bosses. We quit coworkers. We leave clubs and groups and schools and relationships when we don't belong in them or perceive ourselves as not belonging in them. But when we have social support and effective means of working out disagreements, we feel engaged. One of the things I suggest to clients who are going back to school is to organize their cohort for success. Share contact information. Create Google Docs for group note-taking. Share resources. Build a team to help everyone who wants to work together be successful together.

Fairness: This is the perception of equity. Meaning the quality of the procedures in place that impact you and how you are treated in the decision-making process. While nothing can be perfectly fair all the time, the more we can voice that we are striving for that and attending to equity and respect, the better. This means, again, paying people what they are worth. But it also refers to things that don't cost a dime. Like making sure the people without kids get just as many holidays off as the people with kids. And respecting how people want to be addressed (names and pronouns).

Values: These are the ideals and motivation for our engagement. What is the utilitarian exchange in the relationship? In work it is our time and labor in exchange for money and satisfaction and advancement and pride. In volunteer work it's time and labor in exchange for feeling a sense of accomplishment and commitment to change. When the values we are committed to aren't in line with what we're doing, the sense of burnout increases. I am lucky to have a job now where I highly value what I do. In the past I had shit jobs where the job itself was . . . fine . . . but it was food service and I didn't value it in and of itself. But I did value my relationships within it. I valued my relationships with my co-workers and individuals I supervised. I valued my relationships with my customers, especially my regulars. Like the pregnant lady who had a specific tuna-and-pickle sandwich concoction that I fixed for her several times a week and we chatted each time and became friends. There are many different ways of connecting to our value systems in different situations, and it makes all the difference in the world when we can.

Questions for Consideration

> If these six domains add up to engagement, which are most lacking in your life at the moment? If more than one, which is the most pressing issue / most emotionally distressing?
>
> Which aspects of this domain are out of your control?
>
> Which aspects are in your control?
>
> Who are your definite allies in creating change?
>
> Who are your maybe allies in creating change?
>
> What other advantages do you and your allies have on your side?
>
> Idea-dump time: What are all the possible ways you (and your allies) could address strengthening this domain?
>
> Which seems the most doable?
>
> Second idea-dump time: What are all the possible strategies you (and your allies) can think of to approach a structural domain change?
>
> Which seems the most doable?

There you go . . . you have a possible action plan for shoring up a really important area of engagement to ward off (or repair) some burnout in your life in a strategically relational way. That hopefully won't send Agent 626 to the hospital again. Because sometimes changing ourselves and our responses isn't enough . . . sometimes the world needs changing, too.

Imposter Syndrome and Self-Sabotage

Those of us who struggle with imposter syndrome struggle with a highly critical inner voice. This is a pervasive and often invisible source of stress, as well as being the result of stress. It's a cycle: over time, we internalize external cues around our inadequacies and failures, and what we are fed becomes what we feed ourselves.

Our own internal dialogue tells us we lack worth. We are more likely to think of all our successes as undeserved and tend to see ourselves as minutes away from being exposed as the fraud we are. This voice leads to emotional distress, depression, anxiety, addictions, distrust, self-criticism, and self-sabotage. These messages are incredibly common. Many people's inner critics make unhelpful comments about their work, like "You'll never be successful, so why even try? No one appreciates how hard you work. You are under too much pressure; you can't handle this stress. All your successes are just luck, you didn't earn them fairly."

Imposter syndrome was first operationalized by researcher Dr. Pauline Rose Clance, based on her work in clinical settings. She defines it as "a psychological phenomenon in which people are unable to internalize their accomplishments." She was initially studying women in high-powered positions during the 1970s and '80s, when this was still fairly rare. While anyone who fails to value their own contributions can view themselves as an imposter, research shows that it is especially prevalent in people who grew up in very dysregulated homes and experienced parental mistreatment. Disorganized attachment styles are incredibly prevalent among individuals with imposter syndrome.

If we have internalized a felt sense of being lucky rather than competent and hardworking, we start exhibiting a constellation of specific characteristics. Maybe not all of them, in every case, but these are the commonalities described in Clance's work.

1. **The imposter cycle:** Mistrusting your abilities leads to either overpreparation or procrastination. Success then becomes a matter of effort or luck instead of skill acquisition over time.

2. **The need to be the best:** Many people with imposter syndrome found themselves often being the best in certain activities (school, sports, hobbies) growing up. As they move into larger spaces (college, workforce) they bump into other people that are better at certain things, which leads them to disregard how good they are because there is someone better . . . therefore they must be nothing.

3. **Superhuman aspects:** This need to be Superman/ Superwoman/Superperson relates to the need to be the best in that it is about the enormous pressure we exert on ourselves. The difference here is that the need to be superhuman is more about perfectionism than being the best. You may have been the best in some instance but still feel that you didn't do as well as you should have, or that you fucked up in some way by not being perfect.

4. **Fear of failure:** If one needs to be the best, or even perfect, this leads to abject fear around all performance-based tasks. This creates a cycle of overwork, overpreparation, and complete exhaustion.

5. **Denial of competence and discounting praise:** What happens next? We know how hard we (over)worked and attribute all of our success to this fact, which keeps us from accepting positive feedback and praise. This isn't a false humility, but a true discomfort with our own success because we truly don't feel we deserve praise or any of our achievements, to the point we will argue with those who feel otherwise.

6. **Fear and guilt about success:** Because people with imposter syndrome truly feel undeserving, success either feels unearned or leads to anxiety that more will be expected of you, when you are already overpreparing and are entirely exhausted by everything you produce.

We can't talk about imposter syndrome without talking about self-sabotage, can we? While many people with imposter syndrome continue to perform at extreme levels, others of us set ourselves up for failure again and again in preconscious ways. Psychologist Brad Brenner defines self-sabotage as any behaviors where we create harm and destruction around our own well-being and success. Karen Berg, who wrote *Your Self-Sabotage Survival Guide*, agrees, adding that it is the *direct result* of other negative mindsets (like, you know, imposter syndrome). Where imposter syndrome is often correlated with chaotic early childhood experiences and the attachment issues that have emerged from that, self-sabotage is often related to childhood trauma. It can show up as:

- Disorganization
- Indecisiveness
- Perfectionism
- Procrastination

Losing your self-sabotage and imposter syndrome does not mean you'll become a raging egotist or braggart. In fact, it's likely to result in becoming more realistic and even humble. Most importantly, you'll have a clearer understanding of what needs to be done and how your actions and beliefs affect your desired outcomes.

Managing these behaviors, like many mental health efforts, begins with self-awareness. Once we make our preconscious instincts conscious, we can build tools around better managing them.

First things first: Turn yourself into an autoethnographer of your own self-sabotage and imposter syndrome. It is going to feel a little silly to formalize the process, but trust me. You're going to have to formally walk yourself through this process for a bit before it becomes something you do automatically.

Step One: Test your hypothesis that you suck. However much you think you suck? Let's actually find out. Any time you are successful, write that shit down. But you also have to record the relative roles that luck, timing, and your own hard work played in that success. Let's see if that's actually true or if you have more self-agency than you are giving yourself credit for.

Step Two: Pick your cheerleaders. Which people in your life give balanced, accurate, and loving feedback? Check in with them. *Not* with the people who haterade everything you do, or speak only from their own fears. And *also not* the people who tell you the sun shines out of your ass no matter what you say. Real success cheerleaders are the people who have your six in real ways. Ask them. Listen to their answers. Believe them when they tell you you're killing it, not just when they tell you you suck.

Step Three: Model the success of people you admire. And here is the interesting part: You should really admire them. Not just, "Hey, look at the dollar bills this gazillionaire made happen" but, "Look at how this person has held an ethical center and still does great and admirable work while also knocking out some amazing achievements." In neuro-linguistic programming, this is called "success modeling." Look at the people who do shit really well and figure out their strategies. If you can, ask them what's worked for them. And here is the most important part of success modeling: It's not just about watching what they execute perfectly. It's also about watching how they handle failure. How they handle imperfection. How they handle not achieving what they want to achieve and how they learn and grow from those moments.

CHAPTER 9:
BEYOND COPING

Most of this book has focused on the things we need to do in order to make stress more manageable and tolerable. But I wouldn't be me and you wouldn't be you if we weren't both wondering if we could somehow do *more*. Figure out how to make the world a little bit better despite everything. I don't mean that in a spiritual bypassing kind of way, of course. Meaning I don't believe in pretending things are fine when they clearly are not. But I do mean it in the sense that we always have power over our relationship with the world and others, even if the only power we have is in our own response. So what does that look like when we are facing the complexities of our stressed-out lives?

Finding the Pony Skills

You might've heard the parable that these skills get their name from. Basically, it's about a boy who was excited to shovel a large amount of horse manure, because in his view, all that shit meant there *had* to be a pony somewhere. The boy from that story is an example of the type of person who finds the best in every situation. You know those people? Like their car breaks down and they become besties with the tow truck driver? They aren't just

Pollyanna motherfuckers pretending that everything has greater meaning. They are doing something bigger than that. They are taking the reality of their situation and wringing whatever good they can from it. They are saying, "Fuck off world, I'm a survivor." And this is actually using a brilliant fucking coping skill. Finding greater meaning in horrible circumstances allows you to transcend your current environment and leave the world a better place through your advocacy and action.

My favorite book of all time is Viktor Frankl's *Man's Search For Meaning*. His experience as a concentration camp survivor led to a form of therapy known as logotherapy. In a nutshell, he realized that finding meaning can be a fundamental part of our emotional healing. Some coping skills can be transformative as fuck. And that's so badass, don't you think? Let's go over some examples.

Creation

Destruction, as you well know, is not an abstraction. It's a very real entity we cope with on a daily basis. People destroy. They destroy physical structures. They destroy other living beings. They destroy in ways that cannot be measured physically but are physical nonetheless. Anyone who has lain down on the floor from the sheer weight of the awfulness of life can tell you that grief and loss are very real physical things . . . and the reason we can't measure them is because they're far too large for any scale.

What is the antithesis of destruction? Creation. Remember when we talked about the subtle effects of traumatic stress and "little-t" traumas? How they constrict our existence, even inside our own heads? Enlarging our existences again is a powerful way of combating that response.

When other people out there in the world take away from you, create back. Put something into the world that didn't exist before.

There really is no such thing as a "self," no matter what they told you in your psychology classes. But we each have a voice to communicate about everything we think, feel, say, and do. Creation is the sharing of that voice. You can paint a canvas, knit a scarf, play a song, plant a tree, or bake a cake. You can write and write and write and write. On your website, your Facebook, or the back of a napkin at a coffee shop. Creation in the face of destruction doesn't mitigate the loss, but it does help us take back power when we feel completely out of control. You are allowed your voice in the world.

The Tombstone Test

Another easy task, with a perhaps more complicated answer. Think about what you want to see written on your tombstone. Are the things you are doing right now moving you toward that epitaph?

This is another way of asking if what you are doing right now is the way you want to be remembered. If not, how can you shift your behavior so that you are still caring for yourself and maintaining good boundaries but presenting your best self to the world in the process?

Especially in the moments of overwhelm, it is incredibly easy to get wrapped up in what is immediately in front of us. Because paying attention to that makes sense. But it also makes sense to balance that with the bigger picture of who we are, where we are, who we want to be, and where we want to go.

Change the Fucking World

My mom used to make gentle fun of my brother. "Bless his heart, he still thinks he can change the world." My response? "Well, those are the people who usually do." Nobody ever changed anything by sitting around, hoping that people would come to their senses and make better choices. Nobody has gained rights by sitting around patiently waiting for someone to notice that they were getting fucked over.

The writer Anne Lamott writes that when the world overwhelms her, she starts writing checks and planting bulbs. The checks she writes are to organizations doing good work in the world. The ones combating the evil that feels overwhelming to her. Planting bulbs is an investment in the future. Flowers like tulips start as hardy bulbs. They are planted in the fall, and they thrive on spending the cold winter in the ground before flowering in the spring. Planting bulbs acts as a physical reminder that we can survive tough times and bloom anyway.

Things change when we change them. Or, at the very least, we can empower ourselves to fucking *try*. I don't know about you, but I'm not about to sit by and do nothing when the world is on fire. I'll find a bucket of water. Or spit on the fire if that's all I got. But I always feel far better when I try to make things better.

If I'm going down, it's not with an attitude of fatalism and nihilism. I'm fighting each step of the way.

Do Something Nice for Someone

Did you know studies show that doing something nice for someone else activates our reward centers even more than when we do something nice for ourselves? For reals. I'm not saying you can't get yourself a new pair of kicks after a tough week, but consider what you can do for someone else out there who is probably also having a shitty time.

Can you bring muffins in to share with everyone you work with? Compliment a stranger on their cool t-shirt? Shoot hoops with the kids in the neighborhood? Whenever you do something for someone else, you are inviting them into your circle of self-care. And maybe you're giving them permission to start taking better care of themselves and improve their own coping skills.

Practice Compassion and Loving-Kindness

One of the best things we can do for our stress is acknowledge it for what it is with gentleness instead of acrimony. We talked about self-compassion, right? Because compassion starts at home, with our own humanity. Now that we are working on that, we are going to start working on expanding that out to others, and complementing that practice with loving-kindness.

Compassion toward others means wishing that all others be free from suffering. As you work on releasing your own suffering, you also hold this desire for others to have the same freedom. This is a practice you cultivate on a daily basis, not a one-time deal. It's active empathy, without the distancing quality of pity. When we pity someone, we distance ourselves from their experience as not being inherently like our own, rather than accepting that we all hurt and all deserve a release from suffering.

Loving-kindness is the complement of compassion, in that you wish for the positive welfare and happiness of others. It is the opposite of conditional love.

Neither way of living requires being a pushover. You don't have to erase all your boundaries to engage in these practices. You can hold compassion and loving-kindness for people without letting them hurt you. Because after all, isn't the act of hurting others separating them even further from experiencing love and a freedom from suffering?

Pema Chödrön, the Buddhist monk, talks about how hard this practice is, and how even the attempt is very healing. She suggests that in order to take this on, we start with the people we love the most in the world. Compassion and loving-kindness are easy when someone is already your people. Once we are fairly successful in that regard, we move into extending it to the people we aren't so sure about. The people that are a little sketchy. Finally, we move into extending it to the people who hurt us and others the most, and who therefore, in reality, need this the most. The people who we aren't even sure are on Team Humanity at this point.

Holding for them the desire for true happiness and a release of suffering is the greatest gift we can give ourselves, because it frees us of some of their toxicity, if not their actions themselves. It also has a powerful effect on our wellness. It releases harmful stress chemicals, it builds our immune system back up, and it activates the parts of our brain where we process empathy and emotions. In short, caring about the experiences of others makes us better and healthier people, so it is not as entirely selfless a practice as you may think!

Helping Others Cope with Stress (Because No One in the History of Ever Has Calmed Down When Someone Told Them to Calm Down)

You may have picked up this book for yourself, and only yourself. Which makes you a self-care superstar. But a lot of people pick up my books in order to support someone else who is struggling. If that's you, hopefully you've found things in here that are helpful for you in the process of figuring out how to help them. I don't know anyone who couldn't benefit from some more support and tools (and if you know anyone like that, send them my way so I can study them under a microscope!).

The problem with supporting others' ability to cope is that it is so easy to fall into douchebaggery territory by giving them the impression that they are fucked up and need to get their shit together. Even if that is an empirical truth (and exhausting as someone is, chances are the situation is far more complicated than that), telling them that won't get you very far.

Like, literally. Cuz they may slash your tires and then you are really stuck.

A question I get a lot is: How do you approach supporting someone without enabling bad behavior or taking away their autonomy by insisting they do things exactly your way? No one wants to go into one of these conversations being an asshole, but we've all said things the wrong way at some point.

So here are some ideas for lessening the likelihood of a cope-er-vention fail.

- Honor their experience and their emotional response. Anything we feel is valid and real.

- Recognize that no one goes from 0 to 100 instantaneously. They were probably already at 99. They may be good at hiding the fact, or you may have missed the signs, but if it seems like they flipped out at something small, it likely was a proverbial last straw piled on top of everything else they have been trying to manage.

- Without saying you understand exactly how they feel (because no one knows EXACTLY, right?), discuss your own experiences with coping with tough times. Talk about who and what helped you the most. Talk about where you maybe had to recognize that your very real feelings weren't always representative of reality due to your own emotional history and how you shifted your thinking. Elicit hope for the future.

- Give them this book. Show them that DUDE, this is a normal physiological response and they are being badass humans dealing with an exhausted system.

- Help them figure out behavioral chunks you can tackle together that don't feel overwhelming. Maybe you can go over and help them clean up the kitchen. Maybe you can go hiking together. If it is an activity that will benefit the both of you that's all the better, right?

- Remind them that you only want to help if your help is truly beneficial. Don't do unwanted things. Don't make them feel like they have to assign you a task so you can feel useful. Tell them directly, "I do not need to help you to make myself feel better, I want to help you if it will actually help you."

- If they say they don't want help and support, leave the door open for later support. Tell them if anything changes you are available to help and would genuinely like to.

- Get trained in suicide prevention if you haven't already. Be brave in asking those difficult questions. A good training that is all online and will only take an hour of your time can be found here: tinyurl.com/mpsvm65v

Remember that someone may be in a bad place, and their response to their experiences can end up directed toward you. Or toward people you love or care for (like your kids, for example). And hey, you can understand where someone is coming from but not allow bad behavior. Establish boundaries and communicate the consequences of them not being respected. Follow through on the consequences. If contact becomes limited because of these behaviors, communicate what new behaviors you need to see before contact is reestablished.

Healthy Relationship Habits as Stress Inoculation

Remember that pandemic stress research we talked about at the beginning of this book? One of the data points regarding stress during the Covid-19 pandemic was the enormous strain it put on relationships. I can back up this data based on the work I was doing with folks in my private practice during this time period. The people we love the most take most of our hits, no matter what our intention is. I've written in the past about toxic relationship patterns, which can be an enormously helpful tool. Once we are aware of our patterns it is far easier to recognize when we are back on our bullshit so we can make changes and reduce stress for all involved.

But whether we are working through some toxic relational patterns (and honestly we all have them to a varying degree) or we are simply looking for more ways to be skillful in our conversations when we know we are stressed out and not our best selves, these empowering relationship habits, based on the work of Daniel J. Fox, may help. This list isn't designed to shame you with an "ugh . . . you aren't doing anything right" message. In fact, there are tons of things you are doing right, and there are things on this list you are quite likely doing at least most of the time. It is designed to help you reflect on how we often forget to be mindful in our interactions. It gives us some ideas of where we can slow down, reconnect to our mindfulness, and create newer habits that better serve our relationships (which in turn helps mitigate stress). What are you good at? What could you be better at? What skills could you use to improve your communication? What strategies can you put in place to build those skills? While some of these habits are more specific to intimate partnerships, many of them can be applied to relationships of all kinds.

1. **Use as measured and calm a tone as possible.** I know. Yelling at dumbassess is my favorite cardio, too. But weirdly enough, people who need to listen? Don't. While some people handle being yelled at better than others, I don't know anyone who thinks it is an enjoyable experience. And the same percentage of people would likely say it is only adding to an already stressful situation. This isn't to say be all sweet to someone acting salty. It's to say if you keep your volume in a normal range and speak at your normal pace as neutrally as you can, you won't add fuel to the fight. And you'll make it way more likely that the person you are talking to actually receives your message.

2. **Speak in specifics.** Not only will this help people who are neurodivergent and get tangled up when others dance around topics and speak in subtext—it helps EVERYONE. No one is a mindreader. Not knowing what's going on is in-and-of-itself stressful, as we

discussed way back in the stress taxonomy, right? And while some people are better than others at intuiting what you may want, just speaking clearly and plainly will minimize the chance of misunderstanding. I believe the kids call this "ask culture" instead of "guess culture," meaning ask for what you want instead of expecting others to guess what you want.

3. **Demonstrate compassion in your dialogue.** Again, this isn't being all saccharine when someone is showing their ass. It only works if it's real. My clients know it as me being kind over nice. It is our way of saying, "I totally understand how you got to this place, it makes sense to me, you've been doing your absolute best . . . but we have to try something else now, it's time for different skills and better outcomes." People generally really *are* trying their absolute best, and their struggles typically *are* related to their overwhelm/lack of communication skills/lack of self-regulation skills/etc. Perceiving that you're being judged adds to the stress load, and recognizing our human need for compassion can make all the difference in outcome.

4. **Own your fuck-ups.** We all have the idea that the people who never admit their bullshit are the narcissists and gaslighters. Though guess what? Those of us who grew up in homes where mistakes weren't tolerated also really struggle with this. We were trained to live on the defensive because we were raised in a toxic soup of disempowerment. Which is . . . you guessed it . . . really fucking stressful. But in healthy relationships, owning what we got wrong helps others feel that we

are trustworthy and that therefore they can be more open with us. This is *especially* important when the effect of our behavior wasn't near what we intended. We generally go in with good intent and then fumble the pass and *"but I didn't mean to!"* doesn't resolve the other person's pain. Maybe what was funny to you was not funny to your partner, for example. I've been on both sides of that conversation and I bet you have, too. Think of a time when someone was defensive about your hurt feelings and picture what it would have done for you if they had said, "Thank you for telling me how you feel, I never thought of it that way and won't make that joke again." Game changer, right? Heard, understood, valued.

5. **Also, throw in a true apology.** I don't mean "I'm sorry if you are upset," because please don't say that. Just don't apologize if that's all you got. But let's take the above example again. Let's make it "Thank you for telling me how you feel, I never thought of it that way and won't make that joke again. I'm sorry I caused you pain." Notice again we aren't talking about intent, just effect. This apology is attached to your understanding of the other person's experience without defending your intent or telling them they shouldn't feel as they do. It lowers some of the walls that get put up in a stressful situation.

6. **Separate personhood from problems.** Because you are someone who makes mistakes, but is actively seeking to be a better person (cuz you are, right?), presume that's also true of the other people in your life. This habit is directly connected with my in-house relationship rule "the two of you against the problem instead of

the two of you against each other." We are all messy, inconsistent, exhausted, stressed-out humans trying hard to grow in the right direction. Facilitating change doesn't occur by saying "you are shitty and mean" but can occur when you say "I felt hurt when you said [xyz], what I want instead is . . ." We are much more likely to hear someone's feedback (and far more likely to make a change) when it isn't an attack on our personhood. After all, it works better on us, too, right?

7. **Deescalate instead of matching energy.** YKWIM, right? Acting ratchet because your partner is doesn't solve anything. Take a breath, take a pause, and respond wisely and proactively. Same skills used for your own experience of stress. You don't need to win anything or prove anything. Try to see your partner's point of view (this doesn't mean agreeing with it or doing dumb shit because they are insistent . . . I literally only mean *see*). Communicate your disagreement as being about the situation, not the person. But if you are thinking this is how all communication starts with them? No matter how calm you are, they come for you anyway? Then you have other decisions to make about this relationship. And yelling back in the moment doesn't help that decision-making process.

8. **Examine your own chronic unhappy emotions.** What is making you sad, frustrated, irritable, angry, lonely, stressed, etc.? What unmet needs do you have? Can you ask for assistance from another human? If so, communicate these needs with I statements. Meaning, lead with how you feel, not what they did. As in "I felt

anxious and worried when you didn't text me that you were running late. I wasn't upset that you were out with friends, but I like knowing that you're safe if you aren't home when I expected. In the future, can you let me know if your ETA changes?"

9. **Have your own life and things you value outside the relationship.** You are a whole person with or without any partner. Your partner should be your teammate against the fuckery of the world, but that doesn't mean you have to be joined at the hip doing everything together. Have things you like to do. Have things that make you happy and provide you with meaning. It takes a village to manage a stressful existence, right? No one person can be everything to anyone. Your worth shouldn't be solely built around your partner loving you and being happy with you.

10. **Believe in solutions.** When things are tough, believe in your ability to handle them with your partner. Stressful situations feel overwhelming and unsolvable but aren't necessarily. As mentioned above, your partner should be your teammate in the world, not your enemy combatant. Trust the two of you to handle life together, make the best choices you can, and heal. And, also as mentioned above? If your partner doesn't see your relationship the same way? It's time to make a decision about that relationship. You don't have to change your interactions to change your availability for toxic patterns.

The Grenade Test

Quick question: Are the actions you are taking helpful to your relationships? No matter how shitty someone is, responding in kind is essentially lobbing a grenade over the wall. The grenade test is when you step back and ask yourself, "Is what I am about to say or do akin to pitching a grenade at the other person, and at the relationship itself?"

I'm not talking about *allowing* bad behavior from others, I'm talking about *not retaliating* against others for their bad behavior. If people throw grenades at you, replace the pin and hand it back. That may look something like saying, "Hey, that's hurtful and completely not helpful to what we are trying to resolve here. Can we have a productive conversation, or do we need to parking lot this chat until we can respond to each other without striking out?" It may also look like excusing yourself from a diatribe set upon you. But what it *doesn't* look like is fighting back. You don't have to throw a grenade in retaliation to one thrown at you. If you engage in a grenade war, nothing ever gets better because you are still interacting in a way that amplifies the exchange.

Instead, you can take a step back before reacting and decide if you're reacting in a way that serves to make the relationship stronger in the long run. How are your stress responses influencing your thoughts, feelings, and behaviors? How might the other person's stress responses be doing the same? Refusing to fight with someone who's clearly trying to pick a fight better serves the relationship. Adding context to their assholery, rather than reacting with your own, better serves the relationship. Setting a boundary around behavior you will not accept TOTALLY serves the relationship. Punching back just because you got punched does not.

Ask yourself, "What will this response accomplish in both the short and long term?" If the answer is "I'm gonna let a motherfucker know he messed with the wrong person this time!" what does that serve to accomplish in the long term? What if this is your partner, a family member, a dear friend?

You can't force other people to treat you the way you want to be treated (or the way you want the world to be treated), but you can change how you respond. How much power do you want to give them? Do you want to carry that around forever? I don't mean letting people get away with douchebaggery, but I do mean not giving them the power of owning your headspace. Responding appropriately doesn't mean responding with vengeance. Or seething and carrying all those intense, negative feelings for days. You aren't punishing other people with your anger, not really. You're mostly just punishing yourself.

CONCLUSION

O K, so how you doing? That was a lot. Big complicated topic with lots of moving parts and things to consider. Stress is complex, because humans are complex, the world is complex, life is complex. And while this book went over a lot of information about coping with stress, it's super important that you don't beat yourself up for not doing stress well. I don't know if "well" even exists in this situation. The entire engine of modern society operates on the psychic energy of people not doing stress well. The whole game is designed to work that way. If you are exhausted, burned out, depleted, experiencing adrenal fatigue, and the like, just changing your mindset and trying a few quick coping strategies isn't going to resolve all that.

That's why a lot of the advice in this book takes work and time to implement. It took years if not decades to get you to the point of exhaustion you are sitting at right now, right? You can't unfuck this level of attack on a human body by chanting "I'm not stressed, I'm excited!" (though some amount of that can be helpful, as discussed). Caring for yourself and reducing your stress is going to be a constant "(D) all of the above" situation, and it's not going to be a breeze.

But we aren't aiming for well, we are aiming for skillful. And hopefully this book has shown you that becoming a less-fried version of yourself is possible if you take it step by step. You can start by becoming more aware of your own stress response and triggers and using short-term, here-and-now survival strategies to get through what's stressing you out right this very second. Then you can move on up to strengthening your self-care routines, working on your own mindset and relationship to stress, and improving your interactions with others to reduce stress for all. And once you really get going, maybe you'll even transform that stress energy into action toward making the world a better place.

Yes, stress sucks; yes, stress has always sucked; and no, it's not your fault. You're not going to totally get rid of stress, either. But you have the tools to start living with it a little more easily, which can make so many areas of your life a whole lot better. And that is absolutely worth it.

REFERENCES

2022 ICD-10-CM diagnosis code Z73.0. 10. (n.d.). Retrieved May 17, 2022, from icd10data.com/ICD10CM/Codes/Z00-Z99/Z69-Z76/Z73-/Z73.0.

Achor, S. (2011). *The happiness advantage: The seven principles that fuel success and performance at work*. Virgin.

Callinan, S., Johnson, D., & Wells, A. (2015). A randomised controlled study of the effects of the attention training technique on traumatic stress symptoms, emotional attention set shifting and flexibility. *Cognitive Therapy and Research, 39*(1), 4–13.

Cavanagh, M., & Franklin, J. (2000). Attention training and hypochondriasis: Preliminary results of a controlled treatment trial. Paper presented at the World Congress of Cognitive and Behavioral Therapy, Vancouver, Canada.

Center for Deployment Psychology. (2018, March 15). Cognitive behavior therapy for depression.

Chödrön, P. (2018). *The places that scare you: A guide to fearlessness in difficult times*. Shambhala.

Cirillo, F. (2013). *The Pomodoro Technique: Do more and have fun with time management*. FC Garage.

Create Joy and Satisfaction. (2014, February 4). Mental Health America, mentalhealthamerica.net/create-joy-and-satisfaction.

Damasio, A. R. (2003). *Looking for Spinoza: Joy, sorrow, and the feeling brain*. Harcourt.

Do men and women release the same amounts of oxytocin when they are in love? Quora, quora.com/Do-men-and-women-release-the-same-amounts-of-oxytocin-when-they-are-in-love.

Draeger, L. (2013). *Navy SEAL training guide: Mental toughness.* Special Operations Media.

Dupin, L., et al. (2017). Generalized movement representation in haptic perception. *Journal of Experimental Psychology: Human Perception and Performance, 43*(3), 581–595. doi:10.1037/xhp0000327.

Emmons, R. A., & Stern, R. (2013). Gratitude as a psychotherapeutic intervention. *Journal of Clinical Psychology, 69*(8), 846–855. doi.org/10.1002/jclp.22020.

Emotional freedom technique (EFT). Kaiser Permanente. healthy.kaiserpermanente.org/health-wellness/health-encyclopedia/he.emotional-freedom-technique-eft.acl9225.

Fergus, T. A., & Bardeen, J. R. (2016). The attention training technique: A review of a neurobehavioural therapy for emotional disorders. *Cognitive and Behavioral Practice, 23*(4), 502–516.

Fergus, T. A., Wheless, N. E., & Wright, L. C. (2014). The attention training technique, self-focused attention, and anxiety: A laboratory-based component study. *Behaviour Research and Therapy, 61*, 150–155.

Fox, D. J. (2020). *Borderline personality disorder workbook: An integrative program to understand and manage your BPD.* ReadHowYouWant.

Freud, Anna. (1937). *The ego and the mechanisms of defense.* Hogarth Press and Institute of Psycho-Analysis.

Freud, Sigmund. (1894). *The neuro-psychoses of defence.* SE, 3: 41–61.

Freud, Sigmund. (1896). *Further remarks on the neuro-psychoses of defence.* SE, 3: 157–185.

Ganim, B., and Fox, S. (1999). *Visual journaling: Going deeper than words.* Quest Books.

Gewin, V. (2021, March 15). *Pandemic burnout is rampant in academia.* Nature News. Retrieved May 17, 2022, from nature.com/articles/d41586-021-00663-2.

Gowin, J. (2010, October 15). Why Your Brain Needs Water. *Psychology Today*, Sussex Publishers, psychologytoday.com/blog/you-illuminated/201010/why-your-brain-needs-water.

Harper, F. (2010). Walking the good red road: Storytelling in the counseling relationship using the film dreamkeeper. *Journal of Creativity in Mental Health*, *5*(2), 216–220. doi: 10.1080/15401383.2010.485119.

Hofmann, S. G., et al. (2011). Loving-kindness and compassion meditation: Potential for psychological interventions. *Clinical psychology review*, *31*(7), 1126–1132, U.S. National Library of Medicine, ncbi.nlm.nih.gov/pmc/articles/PMC3176989/.

Hollis, J. (2018). *Living an examined life: Wisdom for the second half of the journey*. Sounds True.

Hutmacher, F. (2021). Putting stress in historical context: Why it is important that being stressed out was not a way to be a person 2,000 years ago. *Frontiers in Psychology*, *12*. doi.org/10.3389/fpsyg.2021.539799.

Jordan, J. V. (2018). *Relational-cultural therapy*. American Psychological Association.

Khazan, O. (2022, February 15). Only your boss can cure your burnout. *The Atlantic*. Retrieved May 17, 2022, from theatlantic.com/politics/archive/2021/03/how-tell-if-you-have-burnout/618250/.

Knowles, M. M., Foden, P., El-Deredy, W., & Wells, A. (2016). A systematic review of efficacy of the attention training technique in clinical and nonclinical samples. *Journal of Clinical Psychology*, *72*(10), 999–1025.

Korba, Rodney J. (1990). The rate of inner speech. *Perceptual and Motor Skills*, *71*(3), 1043–1052. doi: 10.2466/pms.1990.71.3.1043.

Koutsimani, P., Montgomery, A., & Georganta, K. (2019). The relationship between burnout, depression, and anxiety: A systematic review and meta-analysis. *Frontiers in Psychology*, *10*. doi.org/10.3389/fpsyg.2019.00284.

Lamott, A. (2006). *Plan B: Further thoughts on faith*. Riverhead Books.

Lazarus, R. S., & Folkman, S. (1984). *Stress, appraisal, and coping.* Springer.

Levauz, M. N., Laroi, F., Offerlin-Meyer, I., Danion, J. M., Van der Linden, M. (2011). The effectiveness of the attention training technique in reducing intrusive thoughts in schizophrenia: A case study. *Clinical Case Studies, 10*(6), 466–484.

Levine, P. A. (1997). *Waking the tiger: Healing trauma.* North Atlantic Books.

Lewis-Fernández, R., Guarnaccia, P. J., Martínez, I. E., Salmán, E., Schmidt, A., & Liebowitz, M. (2002). Comparative phenomenology of ataques de nervios, panic attacks, and panic disorder. *Culture, Medicine and Psychiatry, 26*(2), 199–223. doi. org/10.1023/a:1016349624867.

Liebowitz, M. R., Salmán, E., Jusino, C. M., Garfinkel, R., Street, L., Cárdenas, D. L., Silvestre, J., Fyer, A. J., Carrasco, J. L., & Davies, S. (1994). Ataque de nervios and panic disorder. *The American Journal of Psychiatry, 151*(6), 871–875. doi.org/10.1176/ajp.151.6.871.

Maslach, C. (2017). Burnout: A multidimensional perspective. *Professional Burnout,* 19–32. doi.org/10.4324/9781315227979-3.

Maslach, C., & Leiter, M. P. (2014). *The truth about burnout: How organizations cause personal stress and what to do about it.* Jossey-Bass.

Maslach, C., & Leiter, M. P. (2016). Understanding the burnout experience: Recent research and its implications for psychiatry. *World Psychiatry, 15*(2), 103–111. doi.org/10.1002/wps.20311.

Mohagheghzadeh, A., et al. (2006) Medicinal smokes. *Journal of Ethnopharmacology, 108*(2), 161–184. doi: 10.1016/j.jep.2006.09.005.

Moonshine, C. (2008). *Acquiring competency and achieving proficiency with dialectical behavior therapy.* PESI.

Moore, K. B. (2016, May 16). Does oxytocin give women an edge? It's not quite that simple. *Verily,* verilymag.com/2016/05/oxytocin-sex-differences-women-hormones-bonding-sex-trust.

Moritz, S., Wess, N., Treszl, A., & Jelinek, L. (2011). The attention training technique as an attempt to decrease intrusive thoughts in obsessive-compulsive disorder (OCD): From cognitive theory to practice and back. *Journal of Contemporary Psychotherapy, 41*(3), 135–143.

Murray, J., Theakston, A., & Wells, A. (2016). Can the attention training technique turn one marshmallow into two? Improving children's ability to delay gratification. *Behaviour Research and Therapy, 77*, 34–39.

Nagoski, E., & Nagoski, A. (2020). *Burnout: The secret to unlocking the stress cycle.* Vermilion.

Najavits, L. M. (2003). *Seeking safety: A treatment manual for PTSD and substance abuse.* The Guilford Press.

Nassif, Y., & Wells, A. (2014). Attention training reduces intrusive thoughts cued by a narrative of stressful life events: A controlled study. *Journal of Clinical Psychology, 70*, 510–517.

Oaklander, M. (2016, March 16). Why do we cry? The science of crying. Time, time.com/4254089/science-crying/.

Ober, C., et al. (2014). *Earthing: The most important health discovery ever?* ReadHowYouWant.

Papageorgiou, C., & Wells, A. (1998). Effects of attention training on hypochondriasis: A brief case series. *Psychological Medicine, 28*, 193–200.

Papageorgiou, C., & Wells, A. (2000). Treatment of recurrent major depression with attention training. *Cognitive and Behavioral Practice, 7*, 407–413.

Pappas, S. (2015, June 4). Oxytocin: Facts about the cuddle hormone. *LiveScience*, Purch, livescience.com/42198-what-is-oxytocin.html.

Pendulation, trauma release and bodywork. (2013, August 21). *First of Nine: Tensegrity Blog,* firstofnine.wordpress.com/2011/11/13/pendulation-trauma-release-and-bodywork/.

Porges, S. W. (2011). *The polyvagal theory: neurophysiological foundations of emotions, attachment, communication, and self-regulation.* W. W. Norton.

Robinson, A. M. (2018). Let's talk about stress: History of stress research. *Review of General Psychology, 22*(3), 334–342. doi. org/10.1037/gpr0000137.

Rosenberg, R. S. (2011, July 14). Why you may want to stand like a superhero. *Psychology Today*, Sussex Publishers, psychologytoday. com/blog/the-superheroes/201107/why-you-may-want-stand-superhero.

Samuel, J. (2018). *Grief works: Stories of life, death and surviving*. Doubleday Canada.

Shang. (2022, March 5). Everything you need to know about detached mindfulness. *Metacognitive Therapy Central*. Retrieved April 14, 2023, from metacognitivetherapycentral.com/everything-you-need-to-know-about-detached-mindfulness/.

Shang. (2022, June 4). Why metacognitive therapy is probably the best mental health treatment. *Metacognitive Therapy Central*. Retrieved April 14, 2023, from metacognitivetherapycentral. com/why-metacognitive-therapy-is-the-best-mental-strength-therapy/.

Sharpe, L., Nicholson Perry, K., Rogers, P., Dear, B. F., Nicholas, M. K., & Refshauge, K. (2010). A comparison of the effect of attention training and relaxation on responses to pain. *PAIN, 150*(3), 469–476.

Siegle, G. J., Ghinassi, F., & Thase, M. E. (2008). Neurobehavioral therapies in the 21st century: Summary of an emerging field and an extended example of cognitive control training for depression. *Cognitive Therapy and Research, 31*, 235–262.

Stressors. (2017, August 22). CESH / CSHS. Retrieved April 7, 2023, from humanstress.ca/stress/what-is-stress/stressors/.

Wooll, M. (2022, July 22). Where's your stress from? Learn about different types of stressors. Retrieved April 7, 2023, from betterup. com/blog/types-of-stressors.

Valmaggia, L., Bouman, T. K., & Schuurman, L. (2007). Attention training with auditory hallucinations: A case study. *Cognitive and Behavioral Practice, 14*, 127–133.

Vitamin D and depression. *Vitamin D Council*, vitamindcouncil.org/health-conditions/depression/.

Waxenbaum, J. A., Reddy, V., & Varacallo, M. (Updated 2022, Jul 25). Anatomy, Autonomic Nervous System. *StatPearls*, ncbi.nlm.nih.gov/books/NBK539845/.

Weiten, W., et al. (2018). *Psychology applied to modern life: Adjustment in the 21st century.* Cengage Learning.

Wells, A. (1990). Panic disorder in association with relaxation induced anxiety: An attentional training approach to treatment. *Behavior Therapy, 21*, 273–280.

Wells, A. (2007). The attention training technique: Theory, effects and a metacognitive hypothesis on auditory hallucinations. *Cognitive and Behavioral Practice, 14*, 134–138.

Wells, A. (2009). *Metacognitive therapy for anxiety and depression.* Guilford Press. (Contains the ATT treatment manual for therapists.)

Wells, A., White, J., & Carter, K. (1997). Attention training: Effects on anxiety and beliefs in panic and social phobia. *Clinical Psychology and Psychotherapy, 4*, 226–232.

Yadama, G. N. (1995). Confirmatory factor analysis of the Maslach Burnout Inventory. *Social Work Research, 19*(3). doi.org/10.1093/swr/19.3.184.

Zimmermann, K. A. (2014, February 27). Memory definition & types of memory. *LiveScience*, Purch, livescience.com/43713-memory.html.

ABOUT THE AUTHOR

Faith G. Harper, LPC-S, ACS, ACN, is a badass, funny lady with a PhD. She's a licensed professional counselor, board supervisor, certified sexologist, and applied clinical nutritionist with a private practice and consulting business in San Antonio, TX. She has been an adjunct professor and a TEDx presenter, and proudly identifies as a woman of color and uppity intersectional feminist. She is the author of dozens of books.

MORE BY DR. FAITH

Books

The Autism Partner Handbook (with Joe Biel and Elly Blue)

The Autism Relationships Handbook (with Joe Biel)

Befriend Your Brain

Coping Skills

How to Be Accountable (with Joe Biel)

This Is Your Brain on Depression

Unfuck Your Addiction

Unfuck Your Adulting

Unfuck Your Anger

Unfuck Your Anxiety

Unfuck Your Blow Jobs

Unfuck Your Body

Unfuck Your Boundaries

Unfuck Your Brain

Unfuck Your Cunnilingus

Unfuck Your Friendships

Unfuck Your Grief

Unfuck Your Intimacy

Unfuck Your Worth

Unfuck Your Writing (with Joe Biel)

Woke Parenting (with Bonnie Scott)

Workbooks

Achieve Your Goals

The Autism Relationships Workbook (with Joe Biel)

How to Be Accountable Workbook (with Joe Biel)

Unfuck Your Anger Workbook

Unfuck Your Anxiety Workbook

Unfuck Your Body Workbook

Unfuck Your Boundaries Workbook

Unfuck Your Intimacy Workbook

Unfuck Your Worth Workbook

Unfuck Your Year

Zines

The Autism Handbook (with Joe Biel)

BDSM FAQ

Dating

Defriending

Detox Your Masculinity (with Aaron Sapp)

Emotional Freedom Technique

Getting Over It

How to Find a Therapist

How to Say No

Indigenous Noms

Relationshipping

The Revolution Won't Forget the Holidays

Self-Compassion

Sex Tools

Sexing Yourself

STI FAQ (with Aaron Sapp)

Surviving

This Is Your Brain on Addiction

This Is Your Brain on Grief

This Is Your Brain on PTSD

Unfuck Your Consent

Unfuck Your Forgiveness

Unfuck Your Mental Health Paradigm

Unfuck Your Sleep

Unfuck Your Work

Vision Boarding

Woke Parenting #1–6 (with Bonnie Scott)

Other

Boundaries Conversation Deck

Stress Coping Skills Deck

How Do You Feel Today? (poster)

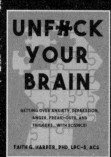

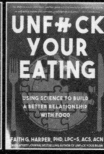

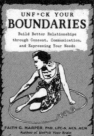